A TREASURY OF

Scottie Dog Collectibles

IDENTIFICATION & VALUES

CANDACE STEN DAVIS

PATRICIA BAUGH

COLLECTOR BOOKS
A Division of Schroeder Publishing Co., Inc.

In this volume we have listed values/price ranges for most items. We have determined these prices from what we have paid or observed in today's market place. The Authors and the Publisher assume no responsibility for any losses which may occur as a result of using values set forth in this volume. Prices we have stated are for an item in excellent or mint condition. Prices should be significantly reduced if an item is damaged or badly worn.

Collectors and sellers should use these values as a guide, not as an absolute. Assigning "book value" to an item is a mistake. Condition, availability, and the desire of the purchaser affect the price of an item; book prices are but suggestions. For example, we have seen Grape Nuts creamers offered from $2 to $50. The amount of joy obtained from possession of the collectible determines the appropriate value! For example, Candace's son made her a lamp when he was 12, and her granddaughter found a small, metal Scottie statue for her, and she wouldn't sell them for any price. Patricia's cousin, Clydean, gave her a stuffed Scottie that was Clydean's childhood toy, and her students, Ryan and Emily Marzolph, have given her a #30 Grape Nuts creamer, salt and pepper shakers, and an autograph book signed by a woman's college friends in the 1930s. These items are priceless to Candace and Patricia. We are certain that there are items in your collection that will never part your company.

Beware of reproductions and unscrupulous dealers who try to offer you a new item that has been "aged." Education is your best defense against these people. When you collect something like Scotties, you must be knowledgeable in every type of collectible as Scotties appear in every medium. Publications such as *Antique and Collector's Reproduction News, Antique Trader,* and *Scottie Sampler* will help you make wise decisions when determining whether an item offered to you is worth the asking price.

Remember, the value of an item is the price most recently agreed upon between the buyer and the seller.

The current values in this book should be used only as a guide. They are not intended to set prices, which vary from one section of the country to another. Auction prices as well as dealer prices vary greatly and are affected by condition as well as demand. Neither the Authors nor the Publisher assumes responsibility for any losses that might be incurred as a result of consulting this guide.

Searching For A Publisher?

We are always looking for knowledgeable people considered to be experts within their fields. If you feel that there is a real need for a book on your collectible subject and have a large comprehensive collection contact Collector Books.

Cover design: Beth Summers
Book design: Kent Henry

Additional copies of this book may be ordered from:

Collector Books
P.O. Box 3009
Paducah, Kentucky 42002-3009

@ $19.95. Add $2.00 for postage and handling.

Contents

Dedications

To my parents for teaching me courage to succeed,
To my husband for giving me love and strength to succeed,
To my children, who have grown and left home, for giving me time to succeed, and
To my grandchildren, the lights of my life, whose love has given me proof of my success.
Candace (Candee) Sten Davis

I dedicate this book to the memory of my mother, Wilabelle Jean Gridley Baugh, who left this world at the age of 32, and to her loving husband, my father, Donald Baugh, the wonderful man who raised my sister, Tammy, and me without the earthly help of his wife. He is truly my hero.
Patricia Baugh

About the Authors

Sixty years ago a young woman agreed to a blind date, but only because she had seen the young man walking two Scotties past her home. They married soon after and twelve years later...

Candace Sten was born and raised in Hyde Park, New York, birthplace of Franklin Delano Roosevelt, owner of the most famous of all Scottish terriers, Fala. Held by Eleanor Roosevelt as a baby, Candace was surrounded by Scottie souvenirs as she grew up. On their honeymoon her husband, Ken Davis, who is also her photographer for this book, bought her a Scottie pin in a small antique shop in New England. Each year he added another to her collection and Scottie collectibles began to appear here and there around their home. Inevitably, one day a live Scottish terrier joined their family. Their second Scottie, Angus Macbeth, is now Candace's real life inspiration, and the Davis home is still acquiring Scottie collectibles.

Candace owns Fancywork, a needlework mail-order business, and she and her husband spend their spare time renovating their 200-year-old home. Candace and Ken have two children, Colleen and Joshua, and two grandchildren, Courtney Moriah and Nicholas Tyler.

Patricia (Patty) Baugh was born and raised in Joy, Illinois, and spent her childhood in the company of dachshunds. She holds degrees in music, and speech and theater, and teaches music and sings professionally, but her passion is collecting. Because of adult onset allergies, she had to live dog-less for many years. While directing the *Wizard of Oz* at a local theater, she kept a cairn terrier, Toto, in her home and found that there was no allergic reaction to him. Now she is kept by two cairns, Toby and Rocky. How does this relate to Scotties? Well, Patricia has always been a collector and became obsessed with the Grape Nuts Scottie creamers because they reminded her of Toby. Fifty creamers later, she has an extensive Scottie collection that grows daily. Toby and Rocky are a bit concerned about the stuffed toys and the doorstops, but other than that, they do not seem to mind the Scottie invasion in their home.

Acknowledgments

We thank the following people for their time, effort, and support for this volume of *A Treasury of Scottie Dog Collectibles*:

Ken Davis, Candee's husband, who spent many hours photographing her collection and the collection of Cheri Hartman.

Cheri Hartman and Sam

Ken Davis

Sharon Ade, Patty's friend, who photographed Patty's collection. Thanks also go to Sharon's husband, David, and their children, Sarah, Rachel, Dan, Tim, and Martha for all their support during the photography sessions. Special thanks go to Sarah for helping with the session and to Martha for modeling.

Patty's father, Don, and her sister and brother-in-law, Tammy Baugh and Mark Swessinger, and her best friend, Susan Mayfield, for their support and love.

To Toby for being Patty's constant companion and to Rocky for keeping her on her toes. Below is Toby at his New Year's Eve Birthday party.

Cynthia Bicker, collector of Scotties and owned by Lucy Belle, who has given her time and efforts to share photographs of her collection for this volume. Cynthia shares her home with Scott Cook — see how far she carries her Scottie obsession!

Toby's birthday party

Angus Macbeth, for all of his "help" during photo sessions.

Cynthia Bicker and Lucy Belle

Angus Macbeth

Cheri Hartman, collector of Scotties and owned by Sam, who has shared part of her collection for this volume. Cheri and her husband Van have three children and two grandchildren.

And last, but not least, we would like to thank our editor, Lisa Stroup, for her kindness and encouragement during the preparation of our first volume of *A Treasury of Scottie Dog Collectibles*.

Introduction

A Treasury of Scottie Dog Collectibles evolved from notes through cyberspace between two Scottie collectors. Shared knowledge and the desire to learn more developed into this volume. We are not experts, simply Scottie collectors like you.

Within these pages you will see hundreds of photographs. The diversity found in this volume, and volumes to come, is unbelievably wide. We hope you enjoy our efforts to bring to you a sampling of Scottie collectibles.

Where to Find Scottie Dog Collectibles

New — Shop everywhere and anywhere. Scotties are used in advertising, in giftware, and on textiles. Most every type of store has, at one time or another, stocked an item with a Scottie representation.

Keep in mind, the giveaways and inexpensive items from 50 years ago are now commanding large prices in antique shops. Your "new" purchases of today will reach antiquity sooner than you think.

Old — Attend garage sales, flea markets, and auctions and look in antique, thrift, and second-hand shops. The items you find may not be in perfect condition and there are several schools of thought on handling antiques. Cleaning an item can cause irreversible damage. If you decide to clean an item, begin in an inconspicuous spot; often water and soap are all that is necessary, followed by a thorough drying. Many collectors feel items shouldn't be touched or repaired as it will devalue your find. Others wish to restore their pieces to their "like new" state. In our opinion, whatever makes you happiest with your collectible is the correct choice.

An important step you should take with your Scottie collection is to document your pieces. Record any markings or history you know, including your purchase price. Photograph your Scotties for insurance purposes. Your efforts will be appreciated in years to come by you and your heirs.

We welcome letters, postcards, e-mail and photographs from our fellow Scottie collectors. If you have history or information about any of the items pictured in this volume, please contact us. We also encourage you to correct any misinformation we have inadvertently published. If you have Scottie collectibles not pictured in this treasury, please share photographs and information for future volumes.

Our addresses are:

Candace Sten Davis
P.O. Box 130
Slaterville Springs, NY 14881
e-mail — fancywork@clarityconnect.com

Patricia Baugh
561 Oaklawn Avenue
E. Moline, IL 61244
e-mail — flamingo@qconline.com

Picture Codes and Arrangement

At the end of each description is a letter code in parentheses. These codes are used to denote owner and photographer of the item, respectively.
(c) Candace Sten Davis; Ken Davis
(p) Patricia Baugh; Sharon Ade
(ch) Cheri Hartman; Ken Davis
(cb) Cynthia Bicker; Cynthia Bicker

We have, in most part, arranged each section according to materials used to create the item. Primarily, items will be shown in the following order: ceramic/plaster/porcelain; composition; glass/metal/wood; and combinations.

Scottie's History

Several hundred years ago the Scottish Highland breeders created a strong, brave little hunter to rout foxes, rodents, and other small creatures. These fellows were the forefathers of today's Scottish terrier. The first recorded Scotties in the United States arrived in 1883, and the present American standard was adopted in 1925. Traits common to the breed include being affectionate, loyal to one person, stubborn, sensitive, courageous, confident, strong, and often comical.

Watch a Scottish terrier jauntily prance across the grass, see the noble stance of this breed in the show ring, witness the fierce commitment when he "goes to ground" after his prey, and chances are you will understand why the Scottie's

image has been used for decades in advertising, fashion accessories, and home decoratives.

The Scottie's silhouette is simple and identifiable, from his "listening" ears to his confident saunter. We can thank FDR's Fala for a wealth of items issued in his image during the 1940s.

According to Corder Campbell of Campbell's Scottish Terriers, the Japanese looked up "brindle" and the definition read "a combination of black and white;" hence many of the Japanese produced Scotties are black and white striped.

Whether they be black, wheaten, or brindled; made of ceramic, composition, glass, metal, or wood; take the form of a decorative or utilitarian object, Scottish terrier items are much sought after collectibles.

The Scottish Terrier Club of America

The Scottish Terrier Club of America was founded in 1900. According to the information found on their web page, their main objectives are: (1) to promote the breeding of pure-bred Scottish terriers; (2) to establish a standard definition of the ideal type of Scottish terrier, known as the "Official Breed Standard," which will assist breeders in their efforts to produce more perfect specimens, exhibitors in their search for likely show ring candidates, judges in their placements of exhibits, and the fancy-at-large in their appreciation of good Scottish terriers; and (3) to advance the interests of the breed by supporting

desirable shows, helping regional Scottish terrier clubs, offering prizes, and encouraging sportsmanlike competition."

The STCA is a non-profit organization. The membership consists of pet owners to breeders to exhibitors, but all have in common the great love for a Scottish terrier.

For more information about the Scottish Terrier Club of America, write to the American Kennel Club, 51 Madison Avenue, New York, NY, 10010, call 212-696-8211 or check out the AKC web site at www.akc.org. They will be able to direct you to the current membership officer of the STCA.

Scottie Dog on the World Wide Web

There is a wealth of information on the Internet, and Scotties have not been neglected. If you have access to a computer, go to a search engine and type in "Scottie" or "Scotty." Plan to spend many hours in front of your monitor as you browse through home pages featuring Scotties, shops featuring Scottie merchandise, and information about the Scottish terrier. There are several Scottie e-mail lists, where people post

information about the breed and chat about their Scottie sightings in the market place.

As a starting point, you may wish to go to Angus MacBeth's web page. Key in this URL address: http://www.clarityconnect.com/web-pages/fancywork/ScottiePage.htm. You'll be greeted by Angus and he'll direct you to many other locations featuring Scotties.

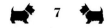

Famous Scotties

Fala

It is a "Fala"cy that advertisers and manufacturers used Scottie representations in the 1930s because of Franklin Delano Roosevelt's dog, Fala.

Fala was born on April 7, 1940. His parents were Peter the Reveller and Keyfield Wendy, owned by Margaret Suckley, a cousin of FDR. This "First Dog" was the constant companion to our 32nd President. He was often found at his master's feet, even during public events.

FDR began "Dogs for Defense." "Dogs" could donate $1.00 to this program and become an official private in the U.S. Army. Fala was the first to join. During its existence, over $75,000 was collected and used to support the working canines helping the war effort. Dogs performed vital duties during this time as sentries, couriers, and bomb detectors. The woods where "soldier dogs" trained at Camp Lejeune, N.C., was called "Fala Woods."

Fala slept in FDR's bedroom and traveled extensively with the President. He had free run of the White House, and it is rumored that since FDR did not want Fala groomed, White House workers would clip bits of fur from Fala's coat as he passed by their desks.

During the 1944 election campaign, FDR's opposition spread the story that Fala was forgotten on an island in the Aleutians and a destroyer was sent to retrieve him at a cost of millions of dollars. In a September speech, FDR responded, "These Republican leaders have not been content with attacks on me, or my wife, or on my sons. No, not content with that, they now include my little dog Fala. Well, of course, I don't resent attacks, and my family doesn't resent attacks, but Fala does resent them. His Scotch soul was furious. He has not been the same dog since."

Fala's life as a Presidential Dog was documented in his biography *The True Story of Fala* by Margaret Suckley and Alice Dalgliesh, originally printed in 1942 by Charles Scribner's Sons. This wonderful book has been recently reprinted by Concepts II Graphics and Printing. Fala was also the subject of numerous newspaper and magazine cartoons.

Fala is the only dog to be included in a Presidential monument in our nation's capitol. The Fala statue is located in the "Third Term Room (1941–1945)" of the four open-air rooms in the FDR Memorial dedicated in May of 1997.

You can see Fala's chair in FDR's Hyde Park bedroom. There is also a display case devoted to him in the FDR Museum, viewed annually by thousands in Hyde Park, New York.

Fala's birthplace, Wilderstein Mansion located in Rhinebeck, New York, is open to the public May through October. This is where Fala also sired two puppies with Button, Heather of Wilderstein.

After FDR's death in April 1945, Fala remained with Eleanor Roosevelt and lived at Val-Kil, her cottage, just a short distance from the family estate in Hyde Park.

Fala passed away April 5, 1952, two days before his 12th birthday. He was laid to rest at his master's side in the Rose Garden at Hyde Park. It was FDR's wish that Fala always be close to him.

Jock

Jock appeared in Disney's animated classic *Lady and The Tramp* of 1955. Generations of movie-goers fell in love with this fellow, even though he only had a supporting role. But like many character actors, Jock made the most of his small part. He has a wonderfully comic song in the beginning of the movie, followed later by a scene where he shows his wise and understanding side. Loyalty to his best friend, Trusty, and tolerance for "wee bairns" who haven't learned proper etiquette with visitors complete his role. Disney Studios gave Jock the opportunity to express typical Scottish terrier personality traits and the animators captured the true bounce and swagger of a Scottie's demeanor. We wish they had given him a starring role after he proved his abilities.

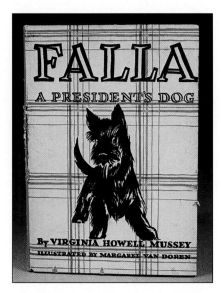

Book, *Falla A President's Dog*, by Virginia Howell Mussey, illustrated by Margaret Van Doren, Howell, Soskin Publishers, copyright 1941. Cannot value as we have only seen one other copy (c).

Coloring Book, *President FDR and Best Friend Fala*, printed by Concept II Graphics and Printing, circa 1997, $5.00 – 8.00 (c).

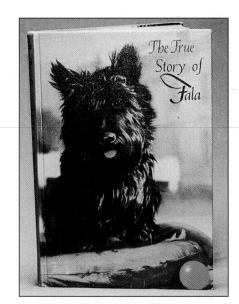

Book, *The True Story of Fala*, by Margaret L. Suckley and Alice Dagliesh, illustrated with sketches by E. N. Fairchild and photograph, Charles Scribner's Sons, New York, 1942, $50.00 – 75.00 (c). This book has been reprinted (1997) by Concept II Graphics and Printing, and is available at Wilderstein and the FDR Museum Shop for $20 hardcover, and $10 paperback. Also available from Scotty's Gifts & Accessories.

Coloring Book, *My Story, the Official Fala Coloring Book*, by Diana Darling, circa 1997, $5.00 – 8.00 (c).

Wooden Scottie with compartment in hinged back, on display at Wilderstein in Rhinebeck, N.Y. Photo courtesy of Wilderstein Preservation.

Photograph of Fala, available from FDR Library Museum Shop.

Wooden Scottie, same as above, with hinged back raised. Photo courtesy of Wilderstein Preservation.

Print, *Fireside Chat*, pencil signed and numbered by artist Marion Needham Krupp, circa 1997, $30.00 – 40.00 (c).

Souvenir and Postcard, 3¼"x4½" glass souvenir marked Hyde Park, New York (Candee was born in Hyde Park and found this in Ohio!); 3½"x5" postcard, marked Alfred Mainzer, 118 E 284th NY 16, circa 1940s, $10.00 – 25.00 (c).

Photograph, Eleanor Roosevelt and Fala, original photo appeared in the December 18, 1951 issue of *Look* magazine.

Postcard, Wilderstein, home where Fala was trained before Margaret Suckley gave him to FDR. He also stayed here when unable to accompany the President on trips. Postcard courtesy of Wilderstein Preservation.

Postcard and Scatter Pin, Fala as he is depicted in the FDR Memorial in Washington D.C., circa 1997, 50¢/$5.95 (c).

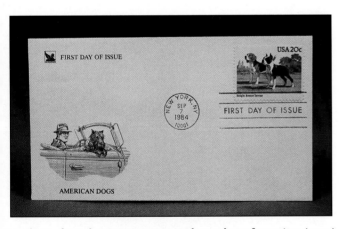

Envelope, first day issue stamp and envelope featuring American Dogs, circa 1984, $6.00 – 10.00 (c).

Christmas Ornament, 3", etched crystal, circa 1997, $30.00 – 40.00 (c).

Medallion, "Fala, FDR's Friend," bronze, circa 1997, $10.00 – 20.00 (c).

Statue, 3"x1¾" plastic, tag printed "Fala," Patty was told by seller that this item was a souvenir item in Washington, D.C. when FDR was in office, $50.00 (p).

Home and Office

Banks

A penny saved is a penny earned.
What better place could there be to save your pennies for your next Scottie collectible?

2½"x2½"x5", ceramic, circa 1940s, $40.00 – 60.00 (c).

2¾"x3¾"x4½", gray metal/painted, circa 1930s, $40.00 – 60.00 (c).

4"x2¾"x5", composition, circa 1930s, $40.00 – 65.00 (c).

2½"x4½"x5", gray metal, circa 1930s, $40.00 – 60.00 (c).

2"x1½"x2", ceramic, circa 1930s, Japan, $50.00 – 75.00 (ch).

"Quin-puplets," 3½"x2½"x4½", gray metal, painted, circa 1936, marked Vanio 36, $70.00 – 100.00 (c).

2½"x3½"x5½", gray metal/painted, circa 1940s, $40.00 – 60.00 (ch).

4"x2¾"x5", composition, circa 1930s, $40.00 – 65.00 (c).

2½"x4½"x5", gray metal/painted, circa 1930s, $40.00 – 65.00 (c).

2¾"x4"x5", gray metal/painted, circa 1930s, $40.00 – 60.00 (c).

6"x5"x2½", brass, circa 1980s, Taiwan, $40.00 – 60.00 (ch).

6½"x4"x6¼", gray metal, circa 1935, marked 1935 Vanio, $40.00 – 65.00 (c).

Bookends

The variety of Scottie bookends is nearly endless. Scotties
make a nice addition to help display your library's editions.
All prices are per pair.

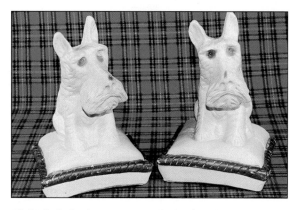

5"x3¾"x6¾", plaster, circa 1940s. $25.00 – 40.00 (c).

4"x5½"x2¼", ceramic, circa 1950s, Japan, Nanco, $25.00 –
45.00 (ch).

5"x3"x6½", plaster, "Cambridge" style, $25.00 – 50.00 (c).

3"x2½"x5", ceramic, circa 1950s, Japan, "Souvenir of
Kingston," $25.00 – 35.00 (c).

5"x3½"x5½", plaster, Italy, $40.00 – 60.00 (c).

5"x2"x5", ceramic, $20.00 – 30.00 (c).

5½"x1"x6½", composition wood, circa 1940s, SyrocoWood $30.00 – 50.00 (c).

5"x2½"x5", composition wood, circa 1940s, SyrocoWood, $35.00 – 50.00 (c).

5"x1"x6½", composition wood, painted, circa 1940s, SyrocoWood, $25.00 – 50.00 (c).

5"x2½"x5", composition wood, circa 1940s, SyrocoWood, $35.00 – 50.00 (c).

4½"x1"x6", composition wood, circa 1940s, SyrocoWood, $25.00 – 50.00 (c).

4½"x1"x6", composition wood/painted, $25.00 – 40.00 (c).

4"x2"x6", composition wood, circa 1940s, $25.00 – 50.00 (ch).

6"x5½"x2½", composition wood, circa 1930s, $20.00 – 35.00 (p).

4"x1½"x5", composition wood, circa 1940s, $25.00 – 50.00 (ch).

5"x3"x6½", clear glass, circa 1940s, Cambridge, $160.00 – 200.00 (c).

6"x5"x3", composition wood, circa 1940s, $25.00 – 50.00 (ch).

5"x3"x6½", black satin glass, circa 1979, made for Cambridge Collector's Club members by Lenox-Imperial Glass Co., marked NCC 1979 LIG, $160.00 – 225.00 (c).

5"x3"x6½", slag glass, circa 1982, made in Cambridge mold by Imperial Glass Co., marked ALIG, $175.00 – 225.00 (c).

4"x3"x5", cast iron/chrome, circa 1930 – 40s, Art deco, $30.00 – 50.00 (c).

5"x2½"x5", metal, circa 1940s, $40.00 – 60.00 (p).

4"x2¾"x6", gray metal/coppery finish, circa 1930s, $50.00 – 75.00 (c).

4½"x2¾"x4¾", cast iron, circa 1940s, "Hubley" style, $100.00 – 150.00 (c).

5½"x2¾"x6", bronze, Galvano Bronze Co., Taunton, Mass., $80.00 – 120.00 (c).

5½"x3½"x5", gray metal/brass painted finish, circa 1934,
Frankart Inc., marked Frankart Inc, Pat. Applied For, $150.00 –
200.00 (c).

4"x3"x5", cast iron/gray metal, $25.00 – 40.00 (c).

4½"x2¾"x5", gray metal/various finishes, circa 1934, Nuart &
Co., marked Nuart Creations NYC, made in US, $40.00 – 60.00
(c).

5½"x2"x5", cast iron/painted (and repainted), circa 1930s,
Hubley, $80.00 – 125.00 (c).

2¼"x3"x4", gray metal/bronze finish, circa 1930s, $50.00 –
80.00 (c).

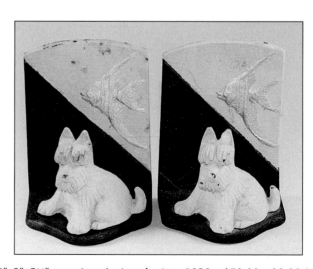

4"x3"x5½", cast iron/painted, circa 1930s, $70.00 – 90.00 (c).

6"x4½"x2", gray metal/marble, circa 1920 – 30s, $65.00 – 100.00 (ch).

4½"x4"x6¼", gray metal/painted, circa 1930 – 40s, $50.00 – 75.00 (c).

6½"x3"x6", cast iron, circa 1930s, $50.00 – 75.00 (ch).

5"x3"x6½", gray metal/various finishes, circa 1929, "Cambridge" style, $35.00 – 55.00 (c).

4½"x3"x5", gray metal/plaster filled, painted, circa 1930s, $40.00 – 60.00 (c).

4"x3"x6", cast iron, circa 1940s, $50.00 – 75.00 (ch).

6½"x2¼"x5", cast iron, circa 1930 – 40s, Hubley, $200.00 – 300.00 (c).

3¼"x3¾"x6½", gray metal/painted finish, circa 1930s, Nuart Co., marked Nuart Creations NYC, $85.00 – 110.00 (c).

3½"x3¾"x4", gray metal, circa 1940s, K&O Co., Made in USA, $30.00 – 50.00 (c).

6"x4½"x2", cast iron, circa 1930s, $60.00 – 85.00 (c).

6"x2"x5½", cast iron, $40.00 – 60.00 (c).

6"x 4¼"x2", bronze, circa 1928, Litco Co., $120.00 – 180.00 (p).

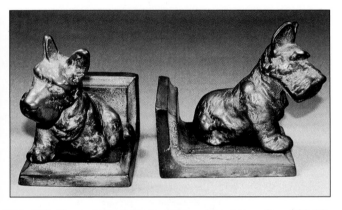

3½"x4¼"x4", cast iron, circa 1920 – 30s, Litco Co., $60.00 – 85.00 (c).

6"x3"x5¾", oak/painted, $40.00 – 75.00 (c).

5½"x2¼"x4¾", cast iron, circa 1929, Connecticut Foundry, marked Scottish Terrier 1929, $120.00 – 140.00 (cb).

5"x3"x6", wood/painted, 1990s, Johann Weih Gmb H, $60.00 – 80.00 (ch).

Desk Top

No self-respecting Scottie would let his or her master work long hours at a desk without being nearby to help. As you will see, Scottie items appearing on the desktop are pretty and practical.

Pencil Sharpener, 1½"x1"x1½", plaster, circa 1980s, $5.00 – 15.00 (c).

Cellophane Tape Holder, 5"x2¼"x4", ceramic, circa 1980s, $10.00 – 20.00 (ch).

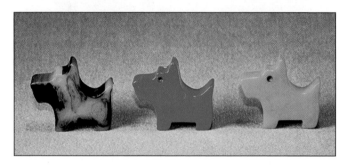

Pencil Sharpeners, 1½"x½"x1¼", Bakelite, circa 1930 – 40s, $30.00 – 60.00 (c).

Stapler, 1½"x1"x3", plaster, circa 1980s, $5.00 – 15.00 (ch).

Pen Holder, 3¾"x2"x3¼", composition wood, circa 1930 – 40s, $25.00 – 50.00 (c).

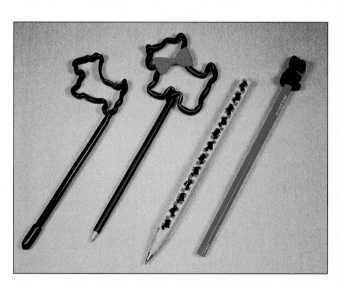

Pens and Pencil, circa 1980 – 90s, $2.00 – 5.00 each (c).

Rocker Ink Blotters, 4"x1¾"x2", left to right: vaseline yellow, jadeite (with clips and blotter), ebony, Houze Convex Glass Company, circa 1930s, $25.00 – 45.00 (p).

Pencil Holders, 2"x1"x2", cast iron, circa 1930s, $25.00 – 45.00 (c).

Paperweight, 2", black milk glass, Souvenir of Scranton, circa 1940s, $10.00 – 20.00 (p).

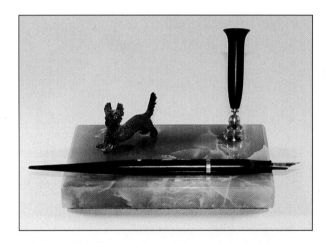

Pen Holder, 6"x3½", marble/cast iron, circa 1940s, $60.00 – 80.00 (c).

Paperweight Pencil Holder, 2¼"x1"x1¾", metal, circa 1930 – 40s, Japan, $25.00 – 50.00 (c).

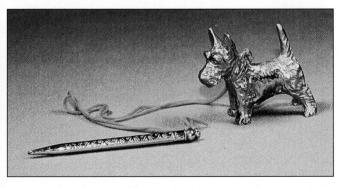

Paperweight Pencil Holder, 2¼"x1"x1¾", metal, circa 1930 – 40s, Japan, $25.00 – 55.00 (c).

Pen Holder, 3"x 3¾", metal/enameled, circa 1930 – 40s, $30.00 – 50.00 (cb).

Pen Holder, 2½", Bakelite/chrome/cast iron, circa 1930 – 40s, $30.00 – 50.00 (p).

Pen Holder, 3"x7", marble/cast iron, circa 1940s, $50.00 – 75.00 (p).

Notepad Holder, 6½"x4½"/Scottie 1¾"x1¾", metal/cast iron, 1930 – 40s, USA, $40.00 – 50.00 (cb).

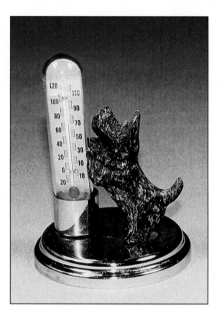

Thermometer, 2½"x3½", cast iron/glass/chrome, circa 1940s, $20.00 – 45.00 (c).

Thermometer, 5½"x3", cast iron, circa 1930s, $90.00 – 110.00 (p).

Letter Opener, 8½"x1"x1½", cast iron/brass, circa 1930s, $25.00 – 40.00 (c).

Letter Box, 9"x3½"x5½", wood/copper, circa 1940s, USA, $25.00 – 40.00 (cb).

Notepad Holder, 5"x7¾", metal, circa 1940s, England, $50.00 – 75.00 (cb).

Letter/Vase Holder (Mystery), 7½"x3"x5", marble/cast iron, circa 1930 – 40s, $200.00 – 250.00 (cb).

Photo Album, 7"x5"x2¼", leatherette, circa 1935, $75.00 – 100.00 (cb).

Pencil Box, 10"x6"x 1½", cardboard/faux leather/gold embossed Scotties, circa 1940s, $20.00 – 30.00 (p).

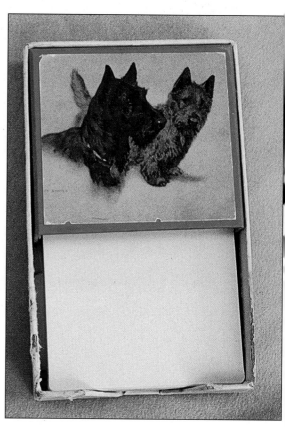

Notepad Holder, 2"x3", cardboard, circa 1940s, $7.00 – 12.00 (p).

Pen/Pencil Holder and Letter Holder, 4½"x5", wood, circa 1960s, $10.00 – 15.00 (p).

Sticky Note Holder, 5"x6", plastic, Sunrise, Inc., Artist: Mary Englebreit, copyright 1996, $12.00 – 15.00 (p).

Doorstops

Here is a group of ever-faithful Scotties
keeping watch over the doors in our homes.

Full-bodied, sitting with glass eyes, 9½"x3½"x8", 3 lbs., composition wood, circa 1940s, SyrocoWood, $50.00 – 85.00 (c).

Hollow-back sleeping, 11½"x2½"x4½", 2lbs., cast iron, circa 1980s – 90s, $10.00 – 25.00. This is a reproduction (c).

5"x11"x12", 4lbs., composition, 1990s, $25.00 – 40.00 (c).

Hollow back, 5"x2"x8", 3 lbs., cast iron, Wilton Products, Inc. Wrightsville, Pa., $60.00 – 85.00 (c).

"Hubley" style full-bodied standing, 10½"x4"x8", 5 lbs., cast iron, circa 1940s, $125.00 – 175.00 (c).

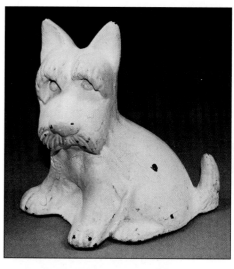

Hollow, 6"x4"x6", 3 lbs., cast iron, $40.00 – 55.00 (c).

"Hubley" style full-bodied standing, 10½"x4"x8", 9 lbs., cast iron, new, $25.00 – 50.00 (c).

Doorstop/bookend, "Listen" style, hollow back, 5½"x2"x5½", 2 lbs., cast iron, circa 1930s, $25.00 – 40.00 (c).

Hollow back sleeping, 11½"x2½"x4", 2 lbs., cast iron, circa 1950s, $30.00 – 50.00 (c).

Doorstop/wedge, hollow back, 4"x4"x5" (width includes wedge), 1 lb., cast iron, new, China, $6.00 – 12.00 (c).

"Listen" style, hollow back, 9"x3"x6", 4 lbs., cast iron, circa 1930s, $75.00 – 110.00 (c).

Hollow back "listen," 8½"x3"x6", 1 lb., painted aluminum, circa 1970s – 90s, $20.00 – 40.00 (c).

Hollow back begging pose, 10"x3"x16½", 8 lbs., cast iron, circa 1930s, $100.00 – 140.00 (c).

11"x9", 11 lbs., Hubley Co., $200.00 – 300.00 (p).

Hollow back begging pose, 9"x3½"x14½", 6 lbs. and 5¼"x2½"x8½", 2lbs., cast iron, new, $15.00 – 30.00 and $10.00 – 25.00 (c).

Lamps
Scotties can definitely light up our lives!

Oil Lamp, 6"x18", glass, circa 1940s, $75.00 – 100.00 (c).

Lamp, 14", ceramic, circa 1940s, $25.00 – 50.00 (p).

Lamp, 4½"x4½"x9", plaster, circa 1930s, $40.00 – 70.00 (c).

Lamp, 8", fired on blue glass/white metal Scotties, circa 1930s, $175.00 – 200.00 (p).

Television Lamp, 12"x8", ceramic, circa 1940s, $45.00 – 60.00 (p).

Lamp, 10", fired on pink glass, Scottie pups in a basket/shades may differ, circa 1930s, $75.00 – 125.00 (p).

Lamp, 10", frosted crystal/metal Scottie, Anchor Hocking Glass Co., circa 1930s, $75.00 – 125.00 (p). There are several versions of this lamp.

Lamp, 10", black amethyst Scottie/frosted crystal shade, circa 1930s, $85.00 – 110.00 (p).

Lamp, 3¾"x12", satin glass, Anchor Hocking Glass Co., circa 1930s, $75.00 – 125.00 (c).

Lamp, 10", clambroth glass with Scottie decals in black or red and black, circa 1930s, $50.00 – 125.00 (p). There are several versions of this lamp.

Lamp, 9"x3"x9", "listen" style, cast iron, circa 1930s, $75.00 – 100.00 (c). Note: Lightbulb, 2¼"x3", glass with filament being a scottie, circa 1940s, $50.00 – 75.00 (c). It still glows when turned on.

Lamp, 6½"x7"x12", gray metal/copper finish, $75.00 – 100.00 (c).

Lamp, 5"x5"x9", gray metal, circa 1930s, $45.00 – 65.00 (c).

Lamp, 6"x4"x6", gray metal/wood, $40.00 – 60.00 (ch).

Lamp, 3½"x6½"x9", gray metal, circa 1930s, "Vanio" style but not marked, $45.00 – 65.00 (c).

Lamp, "Quin-puplets", 2⅝"x2½"x7", gray metal, circa 1936, marked Vanio 36, $50.00 – 75.00 (c).

Lamp, 7¼"x6"x16" (includes shade), gray metal/coppery finish, circa 1930 – 40s, $75.00 – 125.00 (c). This lamp has been altered through time.

Lamp, 5½"x8½", gray metal/satin glass shade, circa 1940s, $50.00 – 75.00 (c).

Lamp, 20", wood, handmade folk art, circa 1970s, $35.00 – 45.00 (p).

Lamp, 3" bulb has neon Scottie which lights when plugged in, metal base, Aerolux Company, circa 1930s, $60.00 – 110.00 (p).

Lamp, 5½"x4"x8", satin glass/cast iron Scottie/celluloid shade, circa 1930 – 40s, $90.00 – 120.00 (cb).

Lamp, 4½"x8"x12", pine, circa 1985, handmade by Candace's son, Joshua, invaluable (c).

Planters

Probably one of the most common items found with a Scottie representation. If all these were used for plants, the Scottie collector's home would be a jungle.

Planter, 4"x2½"x4½", ceramic, circa 1930 – 40s, marked Japan, Darco, Troy, N.Y., $10.00 – 25.00 (c).

Planter, 10"x4"x7½", ceramic, circa 1930 – 40s, $20.00 – 30.00 (c).

Planter, 4"x2½"x4½", ceramic, circa 1940s, marked Japan, Darco, Troy, N.Y., $10.00 – 25.00 (c).

Planters, 4"x3"x4"; 5"x3"x5"; 6"x5"x6"; ceramic, circa 1940s, Japan, $10.00 – 30.00 (c).

Planter, 10"x4"x7½", ceramic, circa 1930 – 40s, $20.00 – 30.00 (c).

Planter, 5"x3"x4½", ceramic, circa 1930 – 40s, Japan, $15.00 – 25.00 (c).

Planter (Pincushion), 3"x1½"x2½", ceramic, $5.00 – 15.00 (c).

Planter, 5"x2½"x3½", ceramic, circa 1940s, Japan, $20.00 – 30.00 (c).

Planter, 7"x3½"x5", ceramic, $10.00 – 20.00 (ch).

Planter, 9"x3"x7", ceramic, $10.00 – 25.00 (c).

Planter, 3"x1½"x2½", ceramic, $5.00 – 10.00 (c).

Planter, 6½"x3"x6", ceramic, $10.00 – 20.00 (c).

Planter, 4½"x2½"x4", ceramic, circa 1940s, Shawnee, $10.00 – 20.00 (ch).

Planter, 8"x4"x8", ceramic, circa 1949, McCoy, $40.00 – 60.00 (c).

Planter, 6"x3¾"x4", ceramic, circa 1940 – 50s, USA 134D, $20.00 – 40.00 (c).

Planter, 3¾"x1½"x3", ceramic, circa 1940s, $10.00 – 20.00 (c).

Planter, 7", ceramic, 1990s, $10.00 – 15.00 (pencil holder on right) (p).

Planter, 7"x4½"x7", ceramic, circa 1953, McCoy, $40.00 – 60.00 (c).

Planter, 2"x3½", porcelain, circa 1930s, Japan, $5.00 – 10.00 (p).

Planter, 8"x8", ceramic, circa 1920s, $15.00 – 20.00 (p).

Vase, 6¼"x4½"x7", ceramic, circa 1940s, $15.00 – 25.00 (c).

Planter/Wall Pocket, 8", ceramic, circa 1940 – 50s, $65.00 – 85.00 (ch).

Planter, 9", ceramic, circa 1930s, Japan, $35.00 – 45.00 (p).

Wall Pocket, 5"x3¼", porcelain, circa 1940s, Japan, $20.00 – 25.00 (p).

Vase, 4¾"x1½"x5", composition wood/glass, circa 1940s, Orna-Wood, $15.00 – 30.00 (c).

Smoking related items are plentiful in the Scottie market place. Possibly FDR's usual appearance with a cigarette and holder helped add to the wide selection of items in this category.

Ashtray, 5"x3½"x3½", china, Beswick, marked 88, Made in England, $85.00 – 100.00 (p).

Pipe Rest, 3½"x3½"x1¾", composition wood, circa 1940s, SyrocoWood, $10.00 – 20.00 (c).

Ashtray/Cigarette Box, body separates for cigarette storage, 5"x3"x5", body ceramic, ashtrays plastic, circa 1980s, $25.00 – 35.00 (ch).

Pipe Rest, 8½"x6½"x3", composition wood, circa 1940s, SyrocoWood, $30.00 – 40.00 (c).

Match Holder, 2"x3", plaster/ceramic, circa 1930s, $10.00 – 15.00 (p).

Pipe Rest, 8"x4"x5", composition wood, circa 1940s, SyrocoWood, $30.00 – 45.00 (ch).

Pipe Holder, 4"x3"x6", composition wood, circa 1940s, SyrocoWood, $25.00 – 45.00 (c).

Ashtray, (glass insert not shown), 4¼"x3"x2½", composition wood, circa 1940s, SyrocoWood, $12.00 – 25.00 (c).

Pipe Holder, 5"x1¾", composition wood, circa 1930s, $15.00 – 20.00 (p).

Ashtray, 5½"x4¾"x3¼", composition wood, circa 1940s, Crest-Wood, $10.00 – 20.00 (c).

Pipe Holder, 3"x3"x6", composition wood, circa 1930s, $20.00 – 25.00 (p).

Ashtray, left: 2"x1", ceramic, circa 1940s, $10.00 – 15.00; Ashtray/Lighter, composition wood, circa 1940s, $20.00 – 30.00 (p).

Ashtray, 7"x5", chalk/glass, circa 1940s, $15.00 – 25.00 (p).

Ashtray/Lighter/Pen Holder, 4"x4"x3½", composition wood base/metal lighter/plastic pen holder, circa 1940s, SyrocoWood?, $25.00 – 55.00 (ch).

Lighter, left: 1"x1", metal, Japan, circa 1940s, $7.00 – 12.00; right: lighter, 2"x3", composition wood/lighter mechanism exposed, circa 1940s, $25.00 – 35.00 (p).

Lighters, left: 2½"x3", composition wood, circa 1940s, $25.00 – 35.00; right: 3"x3", cast iron, Made in Austria, circa 1920s, $45.00 – 55.00 (p).

Above lighters with mechanisms exposed (p).

Lighter, 2½"x1¼"x2¼", composition wood base/metal lighter, circa 1940s, SyrocoWood, $25.00 – 45.00 (c).

Ashtray/Matchbook Holder, 4½"x4½"x3", amethyst glass, circa 1940s, $25.00 – 40.00 (c).

Lighter, 3¾"x3", hollow metal, Zenith, marked Japan, $40.00 – 60.00 (cb).

Ashtray, 4"x1¼", glass, $5.00 – 15.00 (c).

Match Safe, 1½"x1½", metal, circa 1930 – 40s, MatchKing, marked Chicago USA, $40.00 – 55.00 (cb).

Matchbook, left: circa 1930s, $5.00 – 10.00; right: Pocket Lighter, 1"x1", circa 1940s, $10.00 – 12.00 (p).

Ashtray, 6¼"x4"x4", metal, circa 1930s, marked Nuart NYC, $40.00 – 60.00 (c).

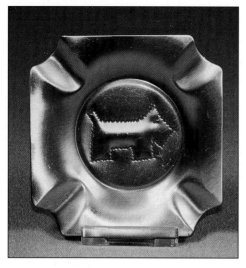

Ashtray, 3"x3", copper, circa 1940s, $5.00 – 15.00 (c).

Smoking Set, Ashtray/Cigarette Box, Match Safe, in original box, metal, Japan, $60.00 – 80.00 (c).

Ashtray, water baffle in base allows Scottie to extinguish cigarettes "nature's way", 5½"x4"x4", metal, marked Runt Ashtray Patent Pending, Scottie marked Sterling Art Metal Wks. LIS City NY, $50.00 – 75.00 (c).

Ashtray, 2½"x2½"x3", metal, circa 1940s, $20.00 – 35.00 (ch).

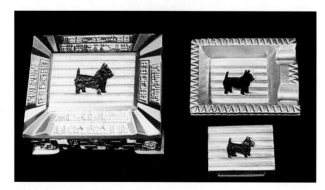

Smoking Set, Cigarette box/Ashtray/Match Case, metal, circa 1930s, $40.00 – 45.00 (p).

Ashtray/Coaster, 5"x3¾", metal, $4.00 – 8.00 (c).

Ashtray, 6"x4", metal, circa 1940s, $20.00 – 30.00 (c).

Ashtray, 6"x4"x3½", cast iron, circa 1930 – 40s, $25.00 – 40.00 (c).

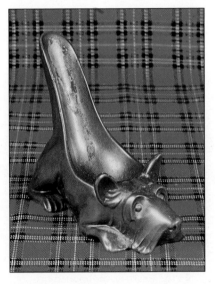

Pipe Holder, 4"x2"x3½", bronze, circa 1930s, marked Des. Pat. 101043, $65.00 – 100.00 (c).

Ashtray, 6"x5", bronze, Nuart, circa 1936, $35.00 – 50.00 (p).

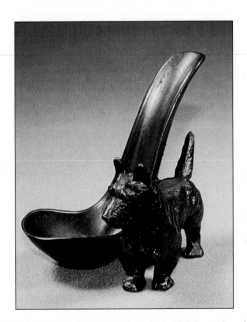

Ashtray, 2½", metal, circa 1940s, $8.00 – 10.00 (p).

Pipe Rest, 3¼"x2½"x3¼", metal, circa 1930 – 40s, $25.00 – 45.00 (c).

Pipe Rest/Ashtray, cast iron, made in Austria, back lifts to expose chamber for ashes/trap door in bottom to empty ashes, circa late 1800s, $90.00 – 125.00 (p).

Cigarette Box, 3¼"x3¼"x1", metal, circa 1930s, Japan, $25.00 – 35.00 (c).

Pipe Rest above, opened (p).

Cigarette Box, 3"x2½"x1½", metal, circa 1930s, Japan, $25.00 – 35.00 (c).

Cigarette Box, mechanical, 4"x2¾"3½", metal, circa 1930 – 40s, Japan, $50.00 – 75.00 (cb).

Cigarette Box, 4"x3¼"x1¾", metal, circa 1930s, Japan, $25.00 – 35.00 (cb).

Cigarette Box, 3½"x3"x2¾", wood, circa 1940s, $25.00 – 35.00 (ch).

Cigarette Case, 2¼"x3½", metal/painted, circa 1930s, $15.00 – 30.00 (c).

Cigarette Box, 6"x4"x3½", wood, circa 1940s, $30.00 – 45.00 (ch).

Cigarette Box, 3"x2½"x3", metal/cast iron, circa 1940s, $10.00 – 20.00 (c).

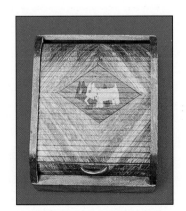

Cigarette Box, 3"x3", wood/inlaid Scotties, circa 1940s, $20.00 – 25.00 (p).

Ashtray, 7"x3½"x4½", wood/glass eyes/plastic, circa 1940s, $20.00 – 40.00 (c).

Ashtray, 6"x3", wood/glass, circa 1940s, $15.00 – 25.00 (p).

Pipe Rest, 3½"x2¼"x3", wood/metal, circa 1940s, $15.00 – 25.00 (c).

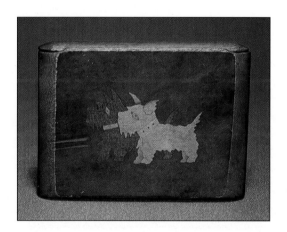

Cigarette Case, 4½"x3¼"x½", wood/inlaid, circa 1930s, $35.00 – 50.00 (c).

Humidor, 4"x8", composition wood/glass, circa 1930s, Dunrite Wood Products, $25.00 – 50.00 (c).

Ashtray, 4"x5"x3", marble/metal, circa 1940s, $15.00 – 25.00 (c).

Ashtray, 5½"x4¼"x4¼", amethyst glass ashtray/metal, Souvenir Shield-Seattle, $45.00 – 65.00 (cb).

Statues

The Scottie's distinct and sturdy appearance makes him the perfect sculptor's model.

3"x7"x4½", porcelain, circa 1980s, marked Beswick England, $125.00 – 150.00 (c).

2"x4½"x4", porcelain, 1990s, marked Goebel Germany, $30.00 – 50.00 (ch).

1"x3½"x3", porcelain, 1990s, marked Beswick England, $30.00 – 50.00 (c).

2½"x1"x2", porcelain, marked Germany, $15.00 – 25.00 (c).

15"x12"x8", porcelain, 1990s, marked Goebel West Germany #3002524, $200.00 – 300.00 (ch).

2½", porcelain, $5.00 – 10.00 (p).

1½" to 2½", china, Japan, $30.00 – 40.00 set (p).

4½"x1½"x3½", porcelain, $15.00 – 25.00 (c).

3½"x2½", ceramic, Japan, $7.00 – 12.00 (p).

2½"x1½"x2½", porcelain, circa 1984 – 85, Department 56, $170.00 – 180.00 (c).

10", ceramic, Japan, marked JK, H227A68, $20.00 – 30.00 (p).

3¼"x5"x3½", porcelain, circa 1980s, Nao by Lladro, $100.00 – 150.00 (c).

4½"x3½"x2", "Jock," ceramic, circa 1980s, marked Disney, Japan, $25.00 – 50.00 (c).

4"x3½", china, Royal Beswick, marked England 804, $125.00 (p).

1½", "Jock", china, Wade, $35.00 – 55.00 (p).

5½"x2½"x4", ceramic, circa 1940s, $40.00 – 50.00 (cb).

3"x1⅛"x2¾", porcelain, 1990s, marked Lochgilphead Scotland, $20.00 – 40.00 (c).

4", ceramic, Japan, $10.00 – 15.00 (p).

1"x1½", composition, circa 1930s, $2.00 – 4.00 (p).

2½"x5"x4", ceramic, 1990s, Theresa's Treasures, $15.00 – 20.00 (c).

2", bone china, $10.00 (p).

8"x3½"x5½", ceramic, 1990s, Theresa's Treasures, $30.00 – 40.00 (c).

10"x6"x9", ceramic, 1990s, $25.00 – 40.00 (ch).

5"x8"x7", ceramic, 1990s, Theresa's Treasures, $25.00 – 35.00 (c).

 50

6¼"x4"x4½", ceramic, 1990s, Theresa's Treasures, $25.00 – 35.00 (c).

5"x2"x3½", ceramic, $15.00 – 20.00 (c).

Doll, 22", ceramic/fabric garment, 1990s, $50.00 – 80.00 (ch).

2½"x5"x4", ceramic, marked Erphila Germany, $20.00 – 40.00 (c).

2½"x3", china, circa 1980s, $40.00 – 60.00 (ch).

3½"x7"x5½", ceramic, marked Erphila Germany, $20.00 – 40.00 (c).

4¾"x2"x3", ceramic, Japan, $10.00 – 20.00 (c).

4½"x3"x6", ceramic, $15.00 – 25.00 (c).

2½"x4½"x4", ceramic, Japan, $20.00 – 30.00 (c).

4½"x1½"x2¾", ceramic, circa 1930 – 40s, Japan, $10.00 – 20.00 (c).

5½"x2¼"x2½", ceramic filled with plaster, circa 1930 – 40s, Japan, $10.00 – 20.00 (c).

¾"x1¼"x1¾", ceramic, Japan, $3.00 – 7.00 each (c).

4½"x1¾"x3", ceramic, marked Marutomaware Made in Japan, $10.00 – 20.00 (c).

1¾"x1"x2½", ceramic, Japan, $10.00 – 15.00 (c).

3½"x2½"x3", ceramic, Japan, $10.00 – 15.00 (c).

3¼"x1"x2", ceramic, Japan, $10.00 – 20.00 (ch).

2¼"x4¼"x3¼", ceramic, Japan, $10.00 – 15.00 (c).

4½"x1½"x3", ceramic, Japan, $10.00 – 25.00 (ch).

2"x¾"x1½", ceramic, Japan, $10.00 – 20.00 (ch).

1" to 2", ceramic, Japan, $5.00 – 15.00 (c).

China, Occupied Japan, second from left has sticker "Souvenir of Canton Ohio," circa 1940s (p).

1" to 2", porcelain, Germany, $10.00 – 20.00 (c).

2½"x3", left: Japan, circa 1940s, $10.00 – 15.00 (p).

2½"x1"x1¾", ceramic, $7.00 – 10.00 (c).

1" to 2", ceramic, Japan, $5.00 – 10.00 (c).

3", china, Japan, circa 1950s, $5.00 – 10.00 (p).

2¼"x2¾", china, marked Scottish Terrier, Royal Doulton K18, Model 1092, circa 1940 – 77, $125.00 – 150.00 (p).

10", carnival chalkware, circa 1940s, $25.00 – 30.00 (p).

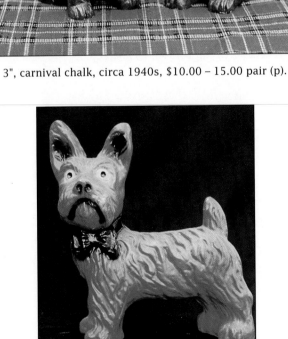

3", carnival chalk, circa 1940s, $10.00 – 15.00 pair (p).

6", carnival chalkware, circa 1940s, $12.00 – 14.00 (p).

10", carnival chalkware, circa 1940s, $30.00 – 40.00 (p).

6", carnival chalkware, circa 1940s, $7.00 – 12.00 (p).

5"x3"x8", carnival chalkware, circa 1940s, $30.00 – 40.00 (ch).

3"x3", carnival chalkware, circa 1940s, $5.00 – 10.00 (p).

6"x2¾"x5½", carnival chalkware, circa 1940s, $15.00 – 25.00 (c).

12"x12"x6", composition, 1990s, $20.00 – 40.00 (ch).

1½" to 2½", chalkware, Japan, circa 1940s, $15.00 – 25.00 (ch).

3", plaster/glass eyes, circa 1984, Stone Critter by United Design, $12.00 – 18.00 (p).

2½", plastic, circa 1940s, $10.00 – 15.00 (p).

2½", celluloid, circa 1920s, $25.00 – 30.00 pair (p).

3", sand, 1990s, $3.00 – 7.00 (p).

10"x8"x9", composition, 1990s, $20.00 – 40.00 (ch).

3½"x1¼"x3", celluloid, circa 1920s, $25.00 – 30.00 pair (c).

2"x1"x2", composition, circa 1930s, $10.00 – 20.00 (c).

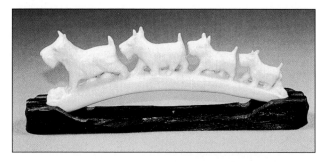

7"x1¼"x2½", plaster filled celluloid, circa 1930s, Japan, $15.00 – 25.00 (c).

4"x8"x6", sand, circa 1980s, marked Sandicast 1985 Sandra Brue, $25.00 – 45.00 (c).

3"x1"x2", plaster filled celluloid, circa 1930s, Japan, $10.00 – 15.00 (c).

2"x3½"x3½", sand, circa 1984, marked Bandanna Sculptures San Diego CA, $15.00 – 20.00 (c).

3¾"x8¾"x6", sand, circa 1980s, $20.00 – 40.00 (c).

4½"x4½"x6", plaster, circa 1930s, $15.00 – 25.00 (c).

7"x3"x5", composition, circa 1983, marked Art Craft Design of S.C., $15.00 – 25.00 (c).

2¼"x2"x3", resin, 1990s, $20.00 – 40.00 (ch).

Left: 3", plaster, 1990s, $5.00 – 10.00; right: 1", composition wood, circa 1930s, $5.00 – 8.00 (p).

3"x7", glass/plaster, $20.00 – 30.00 (p).

Statue 2"x1"x1½", (advertising lipstick display?), ceramic/metallic coated, $10.00 – 20.00 (ch).

2¾"x7"x5½", pecan shell composition, marked Red Mill Mfg., $15.00 – 30.00 (c).

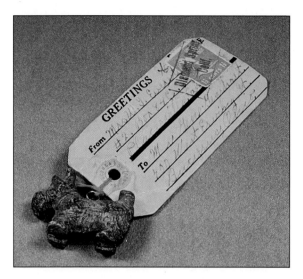

2"x1"x1¼", composition wood, tag attached was used as an address label and it carries a 1½ cent stamp, $25.00 – 40.00 (c).

½" to 1¼", composition wood, circa 1930 – 40s, $5.00 – 15.00 (c).

1¼"x4"x3", composition wood, circa 1940s, $10.00 – 20.00 (c).

2½"x1"x2¼", composition wood, circa 1940s, $8.00 – 12.00 (c).

1½"x4¼"x3¼", composition wood, circa 1940s, $10.00 – 25.00 (c).

5", cast plastic, circa 1950s, $15.00 – 20.00 (p).

1¼", crystal, retired 1996, Swarovski, $75.00 – 100.00 (p).

3"x1"x6", composition wood, circa 1940s, $10.00 – 15.00 (c).

Salt, circa 1930s, $5.00 – 15.00 (p).

3½", glass, crystal/gold opalescence, circa 1960 – 71. Manufactured before Sabino's death in 1971, it is marked with his signature. Item is still being made today, but from 1971 – present, marking is a stamp with his name in block letters. Sabino Art Glass, $100.00 – 125.00 (p).

2" to 4", salt, circa 1930s, $5.00 – 15.00 (ch).

2½"x6"x5", frosted glass, L.E. Smith, $30.00 – 60.00 (c).

2½"x6"x5", black amethyst glass, L.E. Smith, $30.00 – 60.00 (c).

2"x3½"x3", black amethyst glass, circa 1930 – 40s, $25.00 – 50.00 (c).

2½"x6"x5", milk glass, L.E. Smith, $30.00 – 60.00 (c).

JB's, glass by Boyd's Glass Company, (left to right), Row 1: #16 Bermuda Slag, #41 Royal Plum Carnival, #38 Vaseline Carnival; Row 2: #8 Daffodil, #42 Green Bouquet, #43 Mirage, #10 Ebony, #39 Cashmere Pink; Row 3: #1 Cornsilk, #3 Mountain Haze, #4 September Swirl, #44 Purple Frost Slag, #2 Sunburst, circa 1980 – 97, prices vary due to availability (p).

2¼"x¾"x2", glass, L.E. Smith, $5.00 – 10.00 (c).

4", hollow cast iron, circa 1940s, $50.00 – 85.00 (p).

½" to 2", metal (smallest are old Monopoly board game pieces), $1.00 – 15.00 (c).

2"x1½"x2", metal, souvenir plaque on back, circa 1930s, $40.00 – 50.00 (ch).

6"x2"x4", metal, circa 1929, Jennings Bros. Mfg. Co., marked JB 2518, $100.00 – 175.00 (c).

5½"x2½"x3¾", cast iron, $20.00 – 40.00 (c).

3"x1½"x3", metal, circa 1940s, shield Empire State Building NYC, $15.00 – 25.00 (c).

1¾"x4"x3", hollow metal, circa 1930s, $15.00 – 30.00 (c).

 63

3½"x2"x2⅞", metal, wears shield "Kansas City," $10.00 – 20.00 (c).

6½"x3½"x6¼", plaster filled metal, circa 1935, Vanio, $20.00 – 40.00 (c).

6½"x3½"x6¼", plaster filled metal, circa 1935, Vanio, $20.00 – 40.00 (c).

2¼"x1"x2", metal, $10.00 – 20.00 (ch).

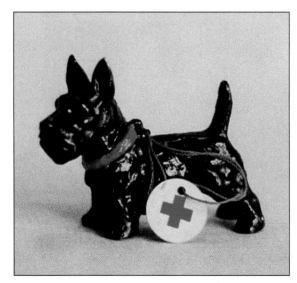

3¼"x2½", tag ⅝", cast iron, circa 1940s, $60.00 – 80.00 (cb). Note: Seller stated this fellow represented Fala during World War II.

4"x3" (frog 1"x¾"), cast iron, circa 1930 – 40s, $125.00 – 175.00 (cb).

6¾"x5", solid bronze, circa 1930 – 40s, $175.00 – 225.00 (cb).

1¼"x3½"x2¼" (including base), marked Hamilton Foundry Quality Castings, Ohio, $25.00 – 45.00 (c).

2"x3½"x3", cast iron, Hubley, $50.00 – 75.00 (c).

3"x1"x2½", metal, circa 1930 – 40s, $10.00 – 20.00 (c).

4"x5", hollow cast bronze, circa 1930s, $35.00 – 55.00 (p).

2½", metal, Germany, circa 1940s, $15.00 – 20.00 (p).

"Listen pair," 7" to 8", metal, circa 1930s, $175.00 – 225.00 (cb).

Gray metal, circa 1930s, $8.00 – 15.00 (p).

6", wax, circa 1920s, $15.00 – 25.00 (p).

5", hollow cast iron, circa 1930s, $35.00 – 55.00 (p).

1½"x1"x2¼", wood, $5.00 – 15.00 (c).

Statue/Bank, 8", rubber, circa 1960s, $5.00 – 10.00 (p).

5", wood frame covered with silk fur, silk hat and scarf, glass eyes, circa early 1900s, Germany, $90.00 – 100.00 (p). (Patty calls him "Pierre.")

12"x6"x8", wood, 1990s, $25.00 – 40.00 (ch).

5", wood, folk art, circa 1980s, $5.00 – 10.00 (p).

4"x½"x3", wood, $15.00 – 25.00 (c).

2¼" and 1", wood, hand carved, circa 1940s, $8.00 – 12.00 (p).

1" to 1½", china/composition, $5.00 – 10.00 (ch).

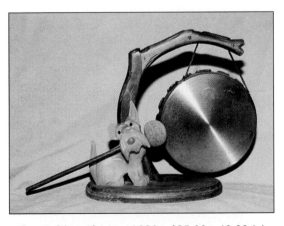

5", wood/metal, circa 1930s, $35.00 – 40.00 (p).

1" to 1½", metal/composition, $5.00 – 10.00 (ch).

Miscellaneous

No matter where you go in a Scottie collector's home, you are bound to find something adorned with this stout-hearted fellow.

Wall Plaque, 6"x6", plaster, $20.00 – 34.00 (ch).

Decorative Plate and Mug, 8", porcelain by Rosalinde, $10.00 – 15.00 each (c).

Thimbles, 1" to 1½", porcelain, $5.00 – 20.00 (ch).

Decorative Plate, 7", ceramic, 1990s, $20.00 – 30.00 (c).

Frame, 4"x5", ceramic, circa 1980s, $5.00 – 15.00 (ch).

Decorative Plate, "International Toasts" Series, 9", porcelain, AmbassadorWare, Founderville, England, $40.00 – 60.00 (cb).

Decorative Plate, 10½", marked Gigi Collector's Edition, $15.00 – 25.00 (c).

Decorative Peg, 11½"x2¾", composition wood, circa 1940s, $20.00 – 30.00 (cb).

Decorative Cup and Saucer, 2¾"x3¼"x5½", bone china, England, $30.00 – 40.00 (cb).

Picture Frame with Cynthia Bicker's Lucy, 5"x7", resin, 1990s, $25.00 (cb).

Windchime, ceramic, Russ, $5.00 – 10.00 (p).

Windchimes, 3"x3", 3"x4", resin/ceramic, 1990s, $5.00 – 10.00 (c).

Wall Plaques, 1½"x2", chalk, circa 1940s, $15.00 – 20.00 pair (p).

Bell, 2½"x4", brass, circa 1940s, England, $40.00 – 60.00 (cb).

Wall Plaque, 4"x2½", ceramic, circa 1940 – 50s, $10.00 – 20.00 (c).

Leash Hanger, 5½"x5½", brass, 1990s, offered in Lillian Vernon catalog, $25.00 each (cb).

Wall Plaque, 2½"x3", chalk, circa 1940s, $15.00 – 25.00 (p)
Note: recently reproduced in plastic.

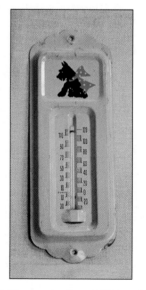

Thermometer, 7½"x3", metal, circa 1930 – 40s, $15.00 – 25.00 (cb).

Kitchen and Entertaining

Not only is a Scottie always ready for dinner (Candee's Angus can attest to that), but Scotties offer their likeness for decoration on everything from cookie jars to tumblers.

Cookie Jar, 12"x10"x7", ceramic, 1990s, $75.00 – 100.00 (ch).

Cookie Jar, 14", ceramic, 1990s, Treasure Craft by Pfaltzgraff, $40.00 – 50.00 (c).

Cookie Jar, 14", ceramic, 1990s, Treasure Craft by Pfaltzgraff, $40.00 – 50.00 (p).

Cookie Jar, 10"x11", ceramic, Metlox, 609 550, Artist: Helen McIntosh, 6/85, $200.00 (p).

 73

Cookie Jar and Original Box, Scotty model DCJ-12B, 11"x6"x8½", ceramic, circa 1980s, marked Marcia Ceramics of CA, Inc., USA, $150.00 – 200.00 (p).

Creamer and Sugar, ceramic, circa 1940s, Morton Potteries, Morton, Illinois, patterned after the Grape Nuts creamer of the 1930s, maroon, $11.00 – 20.00 each (p).

Biscuit Jar, 9¾"x5"x7", ceramic, circa 1980s, marked USA, $75.00 – 125.00 (cb).

Creamers and Sugars, ceramic, circa 1940s, Morton Potteries, yellow, aqua, blue, white, and pink, $11.00 – 20.00 (p).

Cookie Jar, 10"x11", ceramic, Metlox, 607 550, Artist: Helen McIntosh, 6/85, $200.00 (p).

Cereal Bowl, 5", glass, circa 1930s, Hazel Atlas Glass Co., $22.00 – 55.00 (p).

Children's Dishes, ironstone china, circa 1937, marked with a crown and letters C.P. Co. and the numbers 3 37, Crown Pottery and Crown Potteries Company, Evansville, Indiana, USA, 3-piece set, $40.00 – 60.00 (p).

Plate, 6", china, circa 1980s, Department 56, $10.00 – 20.00 (c).

Bowl, 6"x2", pottery, 1990s, Waechtersbach, Germany, $17.00 – 20.00 (ch).

Plate and Bowl, 8" plate/6" bowl, china, marked Home Beautiful C2902 Scotties, Japan, $10.00 – 20.00 each (c).

Children's Dishes, sugar and creamer, glass, circa 1930s, Laurel by McKee Glass Company, $125.00 – 150.00 pair (p).

Napkin Ring, 3"x1"x3", ceramic, 1990s, Japan, $5.00 – 10.00 (c).

Children's Dishes, cup, saucer and plate, glass, circa 1930s, Laurel by McKee Glass Company, 14-piece set, $590.00 – 625.00 (p).

Various ceramic mugs, $5.00 – 15.00 each.

Salt and Pepper, 1½"x1½"x2", ceramic, circa 1930s, Japan, $10.00 – 25.00 (c).

Salt and Pepper, 2"x1"x2", ceramic, 1990s, $3.00 – 10.00 (c).

Salt and Peppers, left, 2", pottery, circa 1932 – 37. It is believed to be Catalina Island Pottery because of glaze, marked 151 on bottom of shakers, $50.00 – 65.00 pair. Right, 1¾", pottery, half a sticker remains and it says vict, with half a crown under that, and cera under the crown, $10.00 – 15.00 (p).

Salt and Pepper, 3½"x4", ceramic, 1990s, $18.00 – 20.00 (ch).

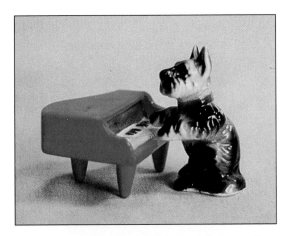

Salt and Pepper, Scottie 1⅜"x3"/piano 2½"x2½"x1½", ceramic, circa 1940s, marked Occupied Japan, $30.00 – 45.00 (cb).

Salt and Pepper, 6", ceramic, 1990s, Treasure Craft by Pfaltz-graff, $15.00 (p).

Salt and Pepper, 1990s, Noritake, "Twas the Night Before Christmas," $20.00 – 24.00 (p).

Napkin Rings, 2¾"x½"x2¼", Bakelite, circa 1940s, $50.00 – 100.00 (c).

Salt and Pepper, 2"x1¼" and 3¼"x1½", ceramic, circa 1940s, marked Occupied Japan, $40.00 – 60.00 (cb).

Spoon, 1"x5", plastic, marked Beetleware 9576, $10.00 – 25.00. Other colors seen: red, blue, green, white.

Trivet, 7"x6", ceramic, 1990s, $10.00 – 20.00 (ch).

Birthday Candle Holder, plastic, circa 1940s, $7.00 – 12.00 (p).

Condiment Shakers, 2⅜"x2⅜"x4½". glass, circa 1940s, Hazel Atlas USA, $30.00 – 50.00 each (cb).

Birthday Candle Holders, 1¾"x1¼", plastic, set of 10, $40.00 – 50.00 (cb).

Silverware with Bakelite Handles, circa 1940s, $25.00 – 50.00 each (cb).

Condiment Shaker, 2⅜"x2⅜"x4¾", glass, circa 1940s, Tipp City USA, $30.00 – 50.00 (cb).

Condiment Shakers, 2"x2"x3", glass, circa 1940s, Tipp City USA, $20.00 – 30.00 each (cb).

Condiment Shakers, 2"x2"x4¼", glass, circa 1940s, Tipp City USA, $60.00 – 90.00 pair (cb).

Beverage Set, glass, 6 glasses/ice tub/swizzle sticks/holder, circa 1930s, Hazel Atlas Glass Company, $125.00 (p).

Glasses, 3", glass, circa 1940s, $5.00 – 15.00 each (c).

Glasses, 5", glass, circa 1940s, $5.00 – 15.00 each (c).

Glasses, 5", glass, circa 1940s, $5.00 – 15.00 each (c).

Glasses, 3", glass, circa 1940s, $5.00 – 15.00 each (c).

Glasses, 3", glass, circa 1940 – 80s, $5.00 – 15.00 each (c).

Glasses, 3", glass, circa 1940s, $5.00 – 15.00 each (c).

Glasses, 3" and 3½", glass, circa 1940s, $5.00 – 15.00 each (c).

Shot Glass and Ice Tub, 1½" glass/5½" bowl, glass, circa 1940s, $5.00 – 15.00/$45.00 – 60.00 (c).

Juice Pitcher, 5"x6", glass, circa 1940s, $25.00 – 40.00 (c).

Ice Tub, 5½", glass, Bartlett-Collins Glass Co., circa 1940s, $45.00 – 60.00 (p).

Pitcher, 9", glass, Bartlett-Collins Glass Co., circa 1940s, $35.00 – 50.00 (p).

Cocktail Shaker, 8", glass, Bartlett-Collins Glass Co., circa 1940s, $40.00 – 60.00 (c).

Decanter, 10", glass, Bartlett-Collins Glass Co., circa 1940s, $75.00 – 100.00 (p).

Creamer, glass, circa 1930s, L.E. Smith, Grape Nuts Cereal Company Give Away, numbers in bottom between back legs 1 thru 37, $5.00 – 40.00.

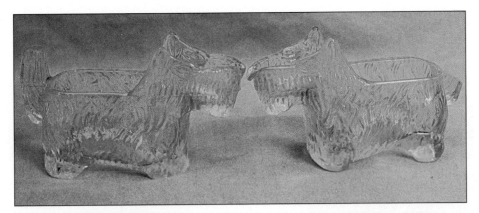

Creamers, glass, circa 1930s, L.E. Smith, Grape Nuts Cereal Company Give Away, colors other than clear are rare, green, $25.00 – 50.00 (p).

Creamer, glass, circa 1930s, L.E. Smith, Grape Nuts Cereal Company Give Away, marigold colored glass; cannot value as we've only seen one.

Baby Bottle, 1½"x2¼"x7", glass, circa 1940s, $40.00 – 60.00 (c).

Cup, 2¼"x2¾", pewter, Rhoda French, $25.00 – 35.00 (cb).

Storage Jar, 5"x6½", glass/plastic lid, 1990s, $2.00 – 5.00 (c).

Storage Jar, 3"x7", glass/plastic lid, 1990s, $2.00 – 5.00 (c).

Chocolate Mold, 5"x2"x5", tin, circa 1980s, $50.00 – 75.00 (c).

Cake Pan, 12"x16"x1½", copper, 1990s, $75.00 – 100.00 (ch).

Cookie Cutters, 3½"x3¼" and 7⅛"x6¼", copper, current, $10.00 – 25.00 (cb).

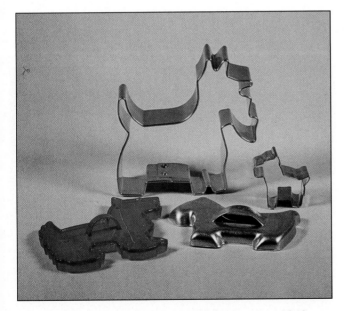

Cookie Cutters, varying sizes, metal/plastic, circa 1940 – present, $2.00 – 15.00 (c).

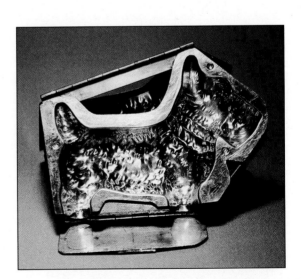

Chocolate Mold, hinged, 7"x4"x8", tin, circa 1940s, $150.00 – 200.00 (c).

Cake Carrier, 11"x10", tin, circa 1950s, $25.00 – 50.00 (c).

Salt or Pepper, 2½"x1"x2¼", metal, circa 1940s, $20.00 – 30.00 pair (c).

Salt and Pepper, 1½"x3¼", metal, $30.00 – 50.00 pair (c).

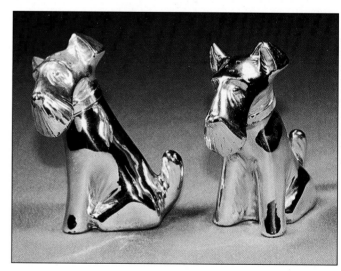

Salt and Pepper, 2"x3", metal, circa 1940s, $25.00 – 40.00 pair (c).

Cork Screw, 3½"x1½", metal, circa 1940 – 50s, $20.00 – 30.00 (cb).

Coasters, 3", metal, circa 1950s, $2.00 – 4.00 each (c).

Tray, 14"x10", tin, circa 1940s, $20.00 – 30.00 (ch).

Crumb Tray, 4"x5", metal, circa 1940s, $15.00 – 25.00 (c).

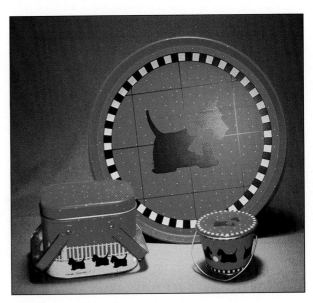

Tray and Tins, 12" tray/4"x6"x4" larger, 3"x3" smaller, tin, circa 1980s, Department 56, $10.00 – 35.00 (c).

Nutcracker, 7"x2½"x7", carved wood, glass eyes, circa 1940s, Germany, $80.00 – 100.00 (c).

Napkin Ring, 3¼"x1⅓"x4", wood, circa 1930s, Italy, $45.00 – 65.00 (c).

Towel Rack, wood, circa 1940s, marked Made in Japan, Souvenir of San Francisco's China Town, $35.00 – 40.00 (p).

Nutcracker, 3"x4½"x7¾", wood, 1990s, Johann Weih Gmb H Germany, $60.00 – 80.00 (ch).

Napkin Holder, 6½"x2½"x3¼", wood with decal, circa 1950s, $20.00 – 30.00 (cb).

Coaster/Tray, 7"x3", composition wood, circa 1940s, $7.00 – 15.00 (c).

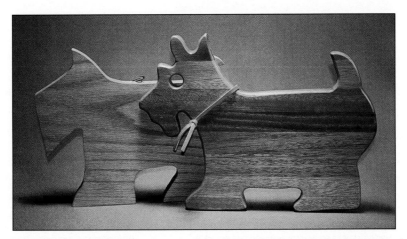

Cutting Boards, 10"x12", wood, 1990s, $20.00 – 30.00 (ch).

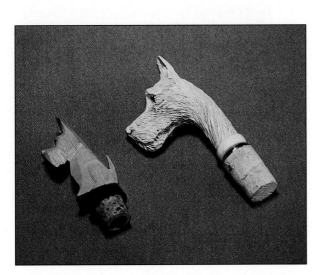

Bottle Stoppers, wood/cork, $15.00 – 35.00 (ch).

Bottle Stopper, ceramic/cork, 1990s, Department 56, $10.00 – 20.00 (c).

Tray, 12"x21", reverse painting on glass/chrome/wood, circa 1940s, $40.00 (p).

Cookie Stamp, 2", glazed stoneware, 1990s, $6.00 – 8.00 (c).

Tray, 11"x19", reverse painting on glass/wood, circa 1940s, Bartlett Collins Glass Co., $30.00 – 45.00 (p).

Paper Plate, 8"x8", paper, circa 1950s, $10.00 – 20.00 (cb).

Bedroom and Bathroom

Our bedrooms and bathrooms offer the perfect places to display and utilize Scottie collectibles. Delicate powder jars, masculine tie racks and many items from other sections are wonderful additions to these two rooms.

Soapdish, Cup, Toothbrush Holder, ceramic, circa 1980s, $10.00 – 15.00 each (ch).

Trinket Box, 6"x3"x7", porcelain, Japan, circa 1950s, $25.00 – 30.00 (p).

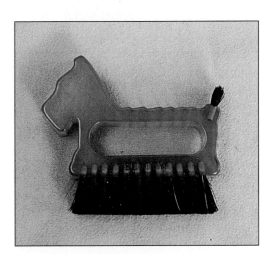

Brush, 3"x2", Bakelite, circa 1940s, $35.00 – 50.00 (p).

Trinket Boxes, 6"x4"x4", ceramic, circa 1940s, $15.00 – 25.00 (p).

Clothes Brush, 3¾"x1½"x4½", composition wood, 1940s, Syro-coWood, $20.00 – 30.00 (cb).

Brush Holder, 5"x3"x6", composition wood, circa 1940s, Syro-coWood, $25.00 – 40.00 (ch).

Clothes Brush, 7", composition wood, SyrocoWood, circa 1940s, $40.00 – 50.00 (p).

Brush Holder (minus brush), 10"x4", composition wood, Syro-coWood, circa 1940s, $20.00 – 40.00 (p).

Tie Rack, 9"x4"x7", composition wood, circa 1940s, Syro-coWood, $20.00 – 40.00 (c).

Tie Rack, 9"x6½"x4", composition wood, circa 1940s, SyrocoWood, $20.00 – 40.00 (c).

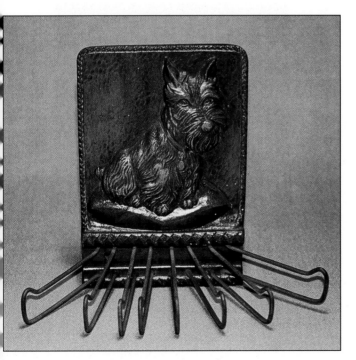

Tie Rack, 4½"x6½"x4", composition wood, circa 1940s, Syro-coWood, $20.00 – 40.00 (c).

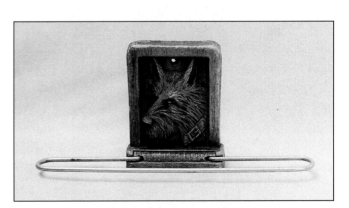

Tie Rack, 4"x8", composition wood, Ornawood, circa 1940s, $15.00– 30.00 (p).

Powder Jar, "My Pet", 4½"x5½", glass, circa 1930s, Diamond Glass Co., $30.00– 50.00 (c).

Bottle, possibly perfume bottle, 2½"x5", glass/handpainted, circa 1940s, $60.00 – 100.00 (c).

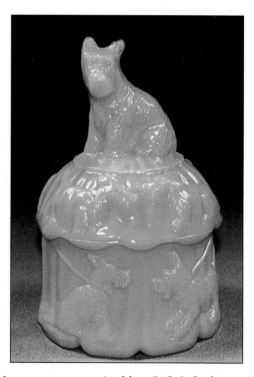

Jar, 2½"x4", glass, circa 1930 – 40s, marked Boric Acid, $20.00 – 30.00 (cb).

Powder Jar, opaque turquoise blue, 3½"x6½", glass, circa 1930 – 40s, Akro Agate, marked Made in U.S. of America and Akro Agate symbol, a crow flying through an A carrying marbles in its beak and claws, $150.00 – 200.00 (c).

Powder Jar, amber, 3½"x6½", glass, circa 1939 – 42, Akro Agate, marked Made in U.S. of America and Akro Agate symbol, a crow flying through an A carrying marbles in its beak and claws, $250.00 – 275.00 (p).

Powder Jar, 3¾"x5½", marigold glass, circa 1930 – 50s, Jeanette Glass Company, $25.00 – 50.00 (c).

Powder Jar, 3¾"x5½", clear glass, circa 1930 – 50s, Jeanette Glass Company, $25.00 – 50.00 (c).

Powder Jar, ice blue, 3½"x6½", glass, circa 1939 – 42, Akro Agate, marked Made in U.S. of America and Akro Agate symbol, a crow flying through an A carrying marbles in its beak and claws, $425.00 – 450.00 (p).

Powder Jar, 3¾"x5½", pink glass, circa 1930 – 50s, Jeanette Glass Company, $25.00 – 50.00 (c).

Powder Jar, 3½"x5", pink glass, circa 1930 – 40s, recessed Scottie in both top and bottom, given with Camay Soap, $20.00 – 40.00 (p).

Candle Holder, Potpourri Jar, Frame, glass/pewter, 1990s, $10.00 – 20.00 each (ch).

Powder Jar, 3½"x5", clear glass, circa 1930 – 40s, recessed Scottie in both top and bottom, given with Camay Soap, $20.00 – 40.00 (c).

Trinket Box, 3"x7", plastic/chrome/cast iron, circa 1940s, $35.00 – 55.00 (p).

Tie Rack, 10"x5", wood/glass eye, Germany, circa 1920, $15.00 – 25.00 (p).

Rack, 10"x3¼", wood, Souvenir of Atlantic City, circa 1940 – 50s, $30.00 – 40.00 (p).

Brush Holder, 2½"x2½"x5", wood, $10.00 – 20.00 (c).

Brush Holder and Shoe Brush, 7", wood/glass eye, circa 1940s, $40.00 – 50.00 (p).

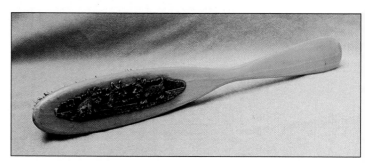

Clothes Brush, 12", wood/composition wood, SyrocoWood, circa 1940s, $20.00 – 30.00 (p).

Perfume Bottle, 2"x1"x2", glass, circa 1970s, Avon, $5.00 – 10.00 (c).

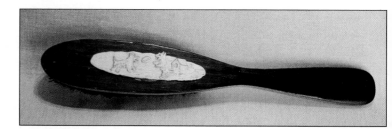

Clothes Brush, 15"x2¼"x1½", wood, circa 1930 – 40s, $20.00 – 40.00 (cb).

Jewelry and Accessories

One of our favorite types of Scottie collectibles is jewelry. Jewelry is an item that consistently appears in every era of the Scottie collectible. From elegant to trendy, what could be more enjoyable than donning Scottie jewelry and heading out the door to shop for more!

Key Rings, 1½" to 2", metal/plastic, circa 1970 – 90s. $8.00 – 20.00 (c). When the Scottie's tail on the far right item is moved, his mouth opens and closes.

Pins, ½" – 1¼", reverse painting on glass, glass/gold/sterling, circa 1930s, $50.00 – 150.00 (c).

Key Ring, 1", metal, circa 1920 – 30s, marked Texaco Western, LISTEN, Utica N.Y., $40.00 – 60.00 (c).

Pins, 1" – 2", enameled metal, 1990s, $20.00 – 40.00 (c).

Pins, ¾" – 1½", sterling/marcasite, circa 1950 – 90s, $25.00 – 50.00 (c).

Pins, 1" – 2", metal, circa 1980 – 90s, $15.00 – 40.00 (c).

Pins, ¾" – 1", sterling/marcasite, circa 1950 – 90s, $25.00 – 50.00 (c).

Pins, 1" – 2", metal, circa 1940 – 50s, $15.00 – 30.00 (c).

Pins, 1" – 1½", metal, circa 1980 – 90s, $15.00 – 25.00 (c).

Pins, 1" – 1½", enameled metal, circa 1940 – 60s, $15.00 – 30.00 (c).

Pins, ¾" – 1", plastic/metal/faux pearls, circa 1960 – 90s, $5.00 – 15.00 (c).

Pins, 1" – 3", metal, circa 1980 – 90s, $15.00 – 40.00 (c).

Pins, 1" – 3", metal/rhinestones, circa 1980 – 90s, $10.00 – 20.00 (c).

Pins, 1" – 2", metal/rhinestones, circa 1950 – 90s, $10.00 – 20.00 (c).

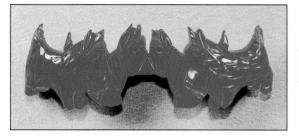

Pin/Scarf Holder, 4", Bakelite, circa 1940s, pin back mounted on bar and pairs of Scotties separate on hinges to fold back and then over a scarf, $200.00 – 300.00 (c).

Pins, 1" – 2", plastic/Bakelite, circa 1940s, left: $5.00 – 15.00; middle: $150.00 – 250.00; right: $25.00 – 40.00 (c).

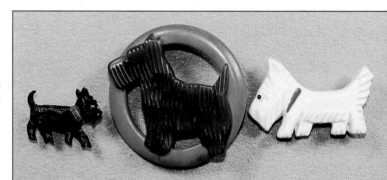

Pins, 1" – 3", Bakelite/plastic, circa 1940s, $20.00 – 50.00 (c).

Pins, 1" – 2", plastic, circa 1940 – 50s, $15.00 – 30.00 (c).

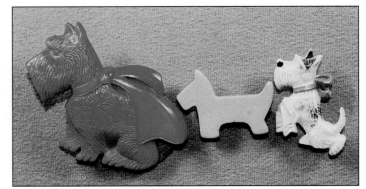

Pins, 1" – 2", plastic, circa 1940 – 80s, $15.00 – 25.00 (c).

Pins, 1¼" – 2", plastic, circa 1940 – 90s, $10.00 – 25.00 (c).

Pins, 1" – 1½", plastic/Bakelite, circa 1940 – 90s, $10.00 – 40.00 (c).

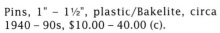

Pins, 2" – 2¼", wood/plastic, circa 1980 – 90s, $10.00 – 20.00 (c).

Pins, 1¼" – 2", wood, circa 1940 – 60s, $10.00 – 20.00 (c).

Pins, 1" – 1½", composition, circa 1940 – 90s, $5.00 – 20.00 (c).

Child's Bracelet, 6", metal, circa 1950s, $15.00 – 25.00 (c).

Child's Bracelet, 6", metal, circa 1950s, $15.00 – 25.00 (c).

Necklace, ¾", pewter, 1990s, $5.00 – 10.00 (c).

Earrings, ¾" – 1", ceramic/metal, circa 1980 – 90s, $10.00 – 15.00 (c).

Charm, ¾", sterling, 1990s, John Joiner from Beatrix Potter, $25.00 – 40.00 (c).

Tie Chain/Clip, metal/sterling reverse painting on glass, circa 1950 – 1990s, $20.00 – 40.00 (c).

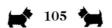

Pins, Row 1 left to right: 1"x2", celluloid, circa 1930s, $20.00 – 25.00; 1½"x2½", composition wood, circa 1940s, $20.00 – 30.00. Row 2 left to right: 1"x1", wood, 1990s, $2.00. 2"x3", celluloid, circa 1930s, $20.00 – 25.00; 1", metal, circa 1960s, $5.00 – 10.00 (p).

Pin, 2½"x2", sequins/glass beads, circa 1940s, $25.00 – 40.00 (cb).

Pin, 1¼"x3¼", Bakelite, circa 1930s, $175.00 (p).

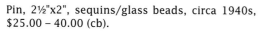

Pin, 2"x2", celluloid, circa 1930s, $7.00 – 12.00 (p).

Pins, top: 2"x2", celluloid, circa 1940s, $20.00 – 30.00; bottom: 7½"x 2½" sweater pin, plastic, circa 1950s, $60.00 – 75.00 (p).

Pins, top: 1", tortoise, circa 1930s, $10.00 – 20.00; bottom left to right: 1½"x1", Bakelite, circa 1930s, $35.00 – 40.00; 1¾"x1½", Bakelite, circa 1930s, $45.00 – 50.00 (p).

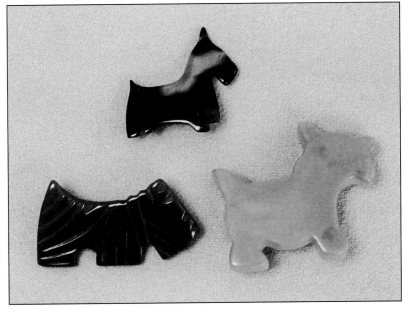

Pins, row 1 left to right: 1¾"x1½", metal/glass/rhinestones, circa 1950s, $10.00, 1½"x1½", metal, circa 1970s, $10.00, 1½"x1", metal/rhinestones, 1990s, $15.00; row 2 left to right: 2¾"x1¾", metal with glass inserts, circa 1950s, $25.00; 2"x2", metal/rhinestones, Trifari, 1990s, $25.00 (p).

Pins, cardboard with various materials used to create designs, Anne Doherty of Moline, Illinois, 1990s, large $18.00, small $12.00 (p).

Pin, 3"x2½", wood/glass eye, circa 1930s, $45.00 (p).

Barrettes, plastic, circa 1980s,
$5.00 – 15.00 each (ch).

Barrettes, plastic, circa 1940s,
$3.00 – 10.00 each (c).

Barrettes, plastic, circa 1950s,
$3.00 – 8.00 each (c).

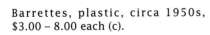

Barrette, metal, circa 1950, $15.00 – 25.00 (c).

Barrette, metal, 1990s, $15.00 – 25.00 (c).

Barrettes, plastic, circa 1981, $1.00 – 5.00
each, on card $8.00 – 20.00 (c).

Barrette, Bakelite, circca 1940s, $30.00 – 50.00 (c).

Barrette, fabric/plastic, circa 1980s, Avon, $5.00 – 15.00 (c).

Compact, 2¼"x⅜", enameled metal, circa 1940s, $30.00 – 50.00 (c).

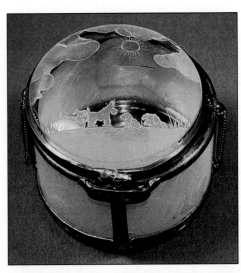

Jewelry Box, 3"x2¼", glass/metal, circa 1991, Foggware, hand engraved optical lenses create lid, mirrored bottom reflects the design to create multiple artistry, $40.00 – 60.00 (c).

Compact, 2¾", metal, circa 1940s, Evans USA, $40.00 – 60.00 (cb).

Child's Purse, 5½"x2½"x3½", vinyl/metal, $15.00 – 25.00 (cb).

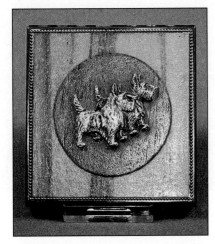

Compact, 3"x3", metal, circa 1940 – 50s, $25.00 – 40.00 (c).

Child's Purse, 5"x2½"x3", leather/celluloid Scottie, circa 1940s, $50.00 – 75.00 (cb).

Glasses Case, 7"x3¾", wool/canvas, 1990s, needlepoint, $10.00 – 15.00 (c).

Child's Purse, 5¾"x2¼",4½", taffeta/metal/plastic handle, circa 1950s, $25.00 – 45.00 (cb).

Purse, 11½"x8" black, 10"x9½"; white, Bakelite/thread, circa 1940s, $60.00 – 125.00 each (cb).

Textiles

Whether you're doing dishes, setting the table, going to bed,
or dressing for the day, Scotties have the situation covered.

Sewing Kit, 3¾"x2¼", satin covered box/metal Scottie, circa 1940s, $30.00 – 50.00 (cb).

Sewing Box, 10"x8½"x8½", wood, circa 1940s, handmade, $50.00 – 80.00 (cb).

Quilt, 48"x60", cotton, 1990s, $80.00 – 125.00 (ch).

Tea Towel, 27"x18", cotton, cross-over collectible found in a display of Black Americana collection, circa 1940s, $35.00 (p).

Towels, cotton, circa 1940s, $10.00 – 20.00 each (ch).

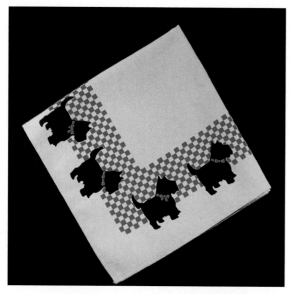

Towel, 16"x28", linen, circa 1950 – 60s, $10.00 – 20.00 (c).

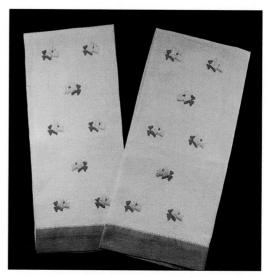

Towel, hand embroidered, linen, circa 1940s, $10.00 – 20.00 each (c).

Towel, hand embroidered, linen, circa 1940s, $10.00 – 20.00 (c).

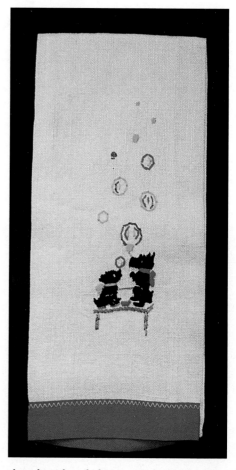

Towel, hand embroidered, linen, circa 1940s, $10.00 – 20.00 (c).

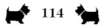

Towels, 19"x14", machine embroidered, linen, circa 1950s, $25.00 pair (p).

Towels & Napkins, hand embroidered, linen, circa 1940s, $10.00 – 20.00 each (ch).

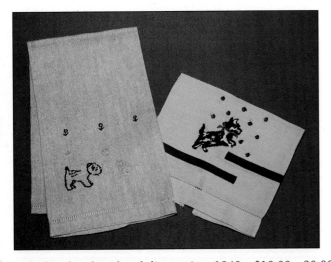

Towels, hand embroidered, linen, circa 1940s, $10.00 – 20.00 each (ch).

Towels, hand embroidered, linen/cotton, circa 1940 – 50s, $10.00 – 20.00 each (ch).

Towels, 19"x14", hand embroidered, linen, circa 1940s, $25.00 pair (p).

Towel, 10"x16", machine embroidered, cotton, 1990s, $7.00 – 10.00 (p).

Towel, cross stitched, terry, circa 1980s, $10.00 – 15.00 (c).

Lipstick cloth, 8"x14", embroidered, $5.00 – 10.00 (c).

Towel, terry, 1990s, $10.00 – 15.00 (c).

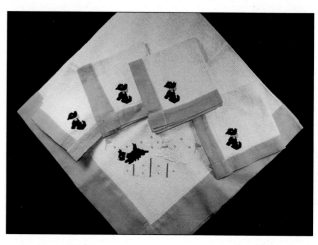

Tablecloth and Napkins, embroidered, 30"x30"/10"x10", linen, circa 1940s, $30.00 – 60.00 (c).

Card Table Cover, 38"x28", linen, circa 1940s, $20.00 – 30.00 (c).

Antimacassar, embroidered, linen, circa 1940s, $15.00 – 30.00 (ch).

Rug, 17"x34", chenille, circa 1940s, $40.00 – 60.00 (c).

Rug, hand hooked, 26"x38", wool, 1990s. Made by Candace with wool hooked on burlap from a kit from Claire Murray. This rug was also available pre-made.

Rug, hand hooked, 25"x42", wool, 1990s, made by Candace with wool hooked on Scottish burlap.

Rug/Tapestry, 20"x40", wool, circa 1950s, $30.00 – 50.00 (p).

Pillow, needlepointed, 12"x18", wool on canvas, 1990s, $60.00 – 80.00 (ch).

Pillow, 8"x12", cotton, hand embroidered, circa 1940s, $10.00 – 25.00 (c).

The Scottish Terrier has a long history that began in the British Isles. In the 17th century, "Scotties" were sent to France as a gift from England. Since then, they have become welcome and useful pets.

Long ago scotties were appreciated for being alert and vigorous hunters. Today they are greatly admired as friendly and loyal pets, devoted to protecting their masters. It is said that the scottie is so dedicated that he will often recognize a master from many years prior, thus making him truly one of man's best friends.

Bottle Bag, 15½"x6", cotton, $10.00 – 20.00 (c).

Skye, a wheaten Scottish terrier, in her Scottie-L T-shirt. Lewallen's Skye Blue resides with Dot and Chris Lewallen, and her brother, Fala Pink, of Columbus, Ohio. She was 6 months old when this photograph was taken, before her first grooming. For those of you who do not "reside" with a Scottie, if you did you would understand why I didn't put Skye was "owned" by Dot and Chris. No one "owns" a Scottie.

Various outfits from the 1990s. Modeled by
Candee's granddaughter, Courtney Moriah
Evans Davis Lauer. She was three-and-a-half
at the time of these photographs.

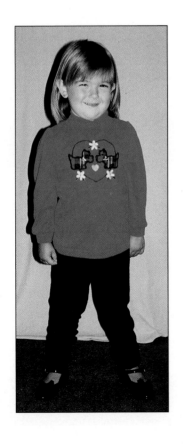

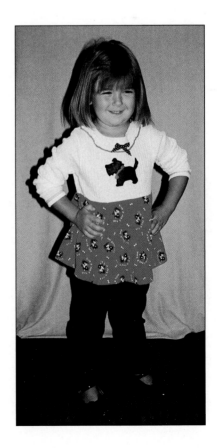

Various outfits from the 1990s. Modeled by Candee's granddaughter, Courtney Moriah Evans Davis Lauer. She was three-and-a-half at the time of these photographs.

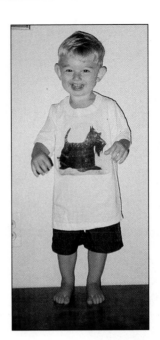

Various shirts from the 1990s, one being the wonderful logo of "Scot's Ahoy" catalog. Modeled by Candee's grandson, Nicholas Tyler Lauer. He was one at the time of these photographs.

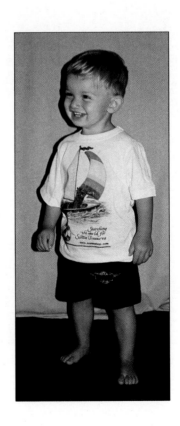

Modeling a Scottie sweatshirt and T-shirt are Candee's daughter, Colleen Lauer, and grandson Nicholas.

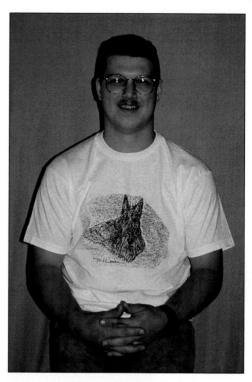

Modeling a Scottie T-shirt from Biscotti's Boutique, is Candee's son-in-law, Jeremy Lauer.

Modeling a Scottie T-shirt from the Tartan Scottie is Candee's son, Joshua.

Modeling a Scottie shirt from Scot's Ahoy is Candee's daughter-in-law, Tammee.

Modeling Scottie T-shirts are Candee's parents, Martin and Virginia Sten, who met in 1937 on a blind date, consented to by Virginia only because she had seen Martin walking two Scotties past her house. They celebrated their 60th wedding anniversary on December 12, 1997. Martin's shirt is from the FDR Museum Shop, located just a few miles from their home.

Dot Lewallen modeling one of her husband's T-shirt designs from Scottie Obsession.

Apron, child's size, appliquéd on cotton, circa 1950s, $15.00 – 25.00 (p). Modeled by Martha Ade, age 7, daughter of Patty's photographer Sharon Ade.

Baby Items, plastic/cotton, $5.00 – 20.00 each, varies per item, (ch).

Hats and Mittens, wool, circa 1980s, $10.00 – 25.00 each (ch).

Socks, cotton, 1990s, $3.00 – 5.00 pair (c).

Child's Hand Muff, corduroy/poly, circa 1980s, $10.00 – 25.00 (ch).

Handkerchief, 9"x9", hand embroidered, circa 1940s, $15.00 (p).

Child's Handkerchief, 8½"x8½", cotton, circa 1940 – 50s, $5.00 – 15.00 (p).

Handkerchief, 13"x13", linen, marked Handkerchief of the month by Burmel as see in *Vogue*, circa 1950s, $25.00 – 35.00 (p).

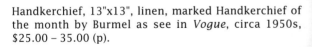 125

Buttons, 1"–2"–1", celluloid/composition wood/celluloid, $10.00 – 30.00 (c).

Buttons, 1½"–1½"–⅞", composition wood, $10.00 – 20.00 (c).

Buttons, 1½"–1"–1½", ceramic/celluloid/Bakelite, $5.00 – 30.00 (c).

Buttons, 1"–¼"–1", plastic/plastic/Bakelite, $3.00 – 5.00 (c).

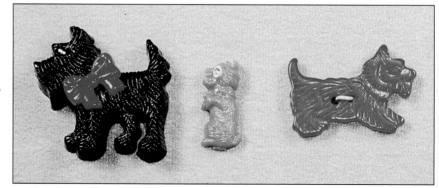

Buttons, 1½"–½"–1", plastic, $3.00 – 10.00 (c).

Buttons, ½", plastic, $2.00 – 5.00 (c).

Buttons, 1"–½"–1", pewter, $5.00 – 10.00 (c).

Buttons, 1"–½"–1", plastic and metal/plastic/metal, $3.00 – 15.00 (c).

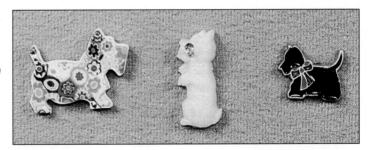

Buttons, ¾"–¼"–½", plastic/plastic/metal, $2.00 – 5.00 (c).

Buttons, 1"–½"–1½", plastic/glass/ceramic, $3.00 – 10.00 (c).

Buttons, ½", reverse painting on glass/pearlized/paper in metal, $5.00 – 20.00 (c).

Buttons. ½", plastic, $3.00 – 7.00 (c).

Buttons, ½", plastic, $3.00 – 7.00 (c).

Buttons, ½", plastic, $3.00 – 7.00 (c).

Buttons, celluloid/except bottom right which is burwood, circa 1940s, $5.00 – 20.00 (c)

Button Card, circa 1950s, $3.00 – 5.00 (p).

Printed Material

Calendars and Advertisements

What better way is there to sell your product than to use an adorable Scottie to do the selling for you? Many manufacturers felt that Scotties were, and still are, great salesmen!

Scottie Calendars, $10.00 – 15.00 (c).

Tin, "Mrs. Steven's Candies," 9", $35.00 – 60.00 (c).

Biscuit Tin, 5"x2", Great Britain, $15.00 – 25.00 (cb).

Pocketknife, 3¼"x½", mother-of-pearl case, Scott Sewing Machine Co. Sample, $40.00 – 50.00 (cb).

Licorice – The Salem Food Company; Tea, Biscuits and Jam – Chesterfields Fine Foods Ltd., 1990s, $5.00 – 10.00 (c).

Biscuit Tin, 4", Great Britain, $15.00 – 25.00 (ch).

Matchbook, circa 1930s, ad for Schuse's Grill in Buffalo, New York, Elvgren art on cover, $5.00 – 10.00 (p).

Shortbread Box, cardboard, 1990s, Maggie Graham's Scottish Shortbread, $5.00 (p).

Chocolate Scotty Dog, 1990s, Niagara Chocolates, $10.00 – 15.00 (ch).

Scotty Beverages Soda Bottle, $10.00 (p).

 131

Texaco, *Ladies' Home Journal*, circa April 1931, Artist: Morgan Dennis, $3.00 – 10.00 (c).

Texaco, circa 1934, $3.00 – 10.00 (c).

Texaco, circa 1934, $3.00 – 10.00 (c).

Kohler of Kohler, *Better Homes and Gardens*, circa August 1925, $3.00 – 10.00 (c).

Kellogg's Grow-Pup, $3.00 – 10.00 (c).

ScotTissue, 10"x13", circa 1942, $4.00 – 7.00 (p).

Friskies Dog Food, 10"x13", circa 1961, $4.00 – 7.00 (p).

Phillips Milk of Magnesia, 10"x13", circa 1947, $4.00 – 7.00 (p).

Champion Spark Plugs, May 1950, $3.00 – 10.00 (c).

Red Heart Dog Food, 10"x13", circa 1941, $4.00 – 7.00 (p).

Greeting Cards and Paper Products

Every era of Scottie collecting has had one thing in common — cards. There is no sunnier greeting than one picturing our beloved Scottie. Included in this section are other paper products as well. Classic to comic, here are some Scottie greetings of yesterday and today.

Various cards from the 1930s – 90s with Scotties helping to express holiday cheer, $5.00 – 20.00 each.

Various cards from the 1930s – 90s with Scotties helping to
express Holiday Cheer, $5.00 – 20.00 each.

Valentine, 5"x2½", paper, $5.00 – 10.00 (c).

Valentine, 4½"x7½", paper, circa 1930s, Germany,
$5.00 – 10.00 (cb).

Postcards, left: *Oliver Twist* by Minnie Keene, England; top right: Switzerland; bottom right: U.S.A., $3.00 – 6.00 each (p).

Greeting Card and Bookmark, "Lady and the Tramp," paper, 1990s, $3.00 – 7.00 (c).

Postcard, made in Asheville, N.C., $2.00 (p).

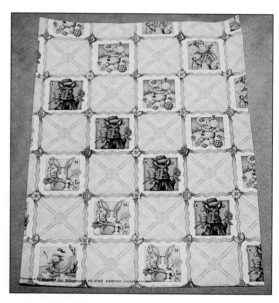

Wrapping paper, Copyright 1996, Sunrise Inc., Artist: Mary Englebreit, $3.00 (p).

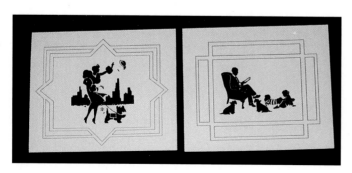

Notecards, 1990s, $6.00 – 10.00 box (c).

Greeting Cards, Copyright 1996, Sunrise, Inc., Artist: Mary Englebreit, $1.00 – 3.00 (p). *Courtesy of Barbara Strother, marketing coordinator, InterArt Distribution. Mary Englebreit items are from Sunrise, Inc.*

Writing Paper and School Supplies, paper/plastic, 1990s, Lisa Frank, $3.00 – 10.00 (c).

Writing Paper, circa 1980s, $5.00 – 15.00 (c).

Greeting Card, Amy and Andy, 1990s, Caspari Ltd., Artist: Constance Coleman, Switzerland, $3.00 – 5.00 (c).

Writing Paper, circa 1980s, $5.00 – 15.00 (c).

Package and Greeting Card, Copyright 1996, Sunrise Inc., Artist: Mary Englebreit, $2.00 (p).

Books and Videos

This is just a small sampling of books available featuring Scotties. We have included a list in the back of this volume of a few more to watch for on your Scottie shopping trips. What better way to use Scottie bookends, than to hold up Scottie books!.

Video, "Angus Lost," based on the book by Marjorie Flack, Goodtimes Home Video Corp., copyright 1995, $10.00 – 15.00

Bookplate, 3"x4", paper, $1.00 – 3.00 each (c).

Comfort, Vol. XLIX No. 6, circa April 1937, $3.00 – 10.00 (c).

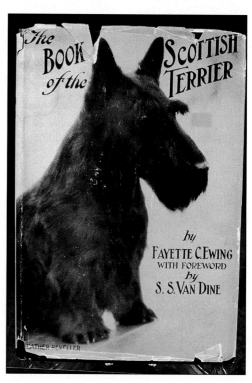

The Book of the Scottish Terrier by Fayette C. Ewing with foreword by S. S. Van Dine, revised edition 1946, $50.00 – 75.00 (c).

Peggy Brown series by Kathryn Keisenfelt, 4½"x3¾"x1½", paperback, circa 1930 – 40s, $20.00 – 40.00 each (cb).

Autograph Book, 6½"x4½", leather/cardboard, circa 1936 – 37. This book belonged to a woman named Irene Licht and it is full of autographs from when she was a student at the Iowa State Teacher's College in Cedar Falls, now known as University of Northern Iowa. It is fascinating and was a gift to Patty from one of the families at her school, priceless.

Autograph Book, 6½"x4½", wooden cover, circa 1940s, $9.00 – 12.00 (p).

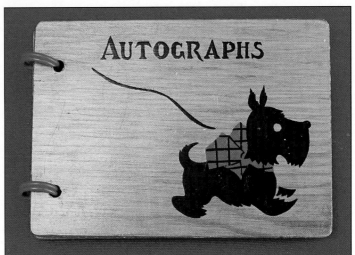

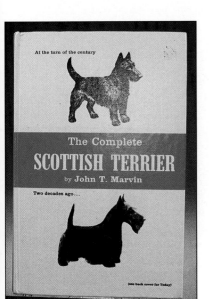

The Complete Scottish Terrier by John T. Marvin, copyright 1967, $10.00 – 20.00 (c).

Bonnie Bits O' Bonnie Scotland, described by Allan Junior, published by Valentine & Sons, Ltd., Dundee & London. Small volume is filled with pictures reproduced in facsimile from original paintings, $5.00 – 10.00 (c).

The Fala Factor by Stuart M. Kaminsky, paperback, circa 1984, Mysterious Press, $10.00 – 20.00 (cb).

Angus and the Ducks by Marjorie Flack, hardcover, circa 1930, Doubleday & Company, Inc., $40.00 – 50.00 (c).

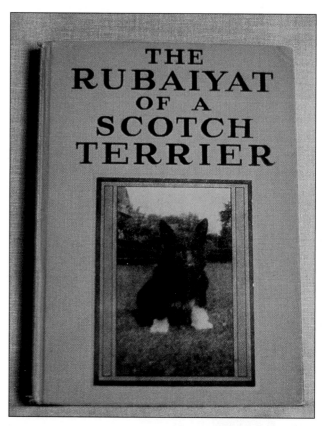

Angus and the Cat by Marjorie Flack, hardcover, circa 1931, Doubleday & Company, Inc., $40.00 – 50.00 (c).

The Rubaiyat of a Scotch Terrier by Sewell Collins, hardcover, circa 1926, F. A. Stokes Co., $30.00 – 50.00 (cb).

Mac Goes to School by Margaret L. Wynkopp, hardback, circa 1942, Doubleday, $40.00 – 60.00 (cb).

Animals, 9"x8", cloth, circa 1940s, Hampton Publishing Company, $15.00 – 25.00 (c).

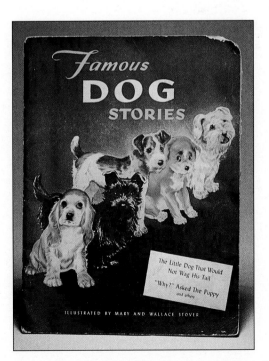

ABC Dogs by Clara Tice, hardcover, reprinted 1995, $15.00 (c).

Famous Dog Stories, illustrated by Mary and Wallace Stover, paperback, circa 1944, $10.00 – 25.00 (c).

Fine Art

The Scottish terrier has been providing artists with a versatile subject for many years. From the renderings of Marguerite Kirmse to today's works of art by Marion Needham Krupp, there are no boundaries on what the Scottie brings to the world of fine art.

Print, "Check and Double Check," 10½"x8", circa 1930, by Grace Drayton, for RKO Studios, marked Buddies, a Reliance Product, $40.00 – 50.00 (c).

Print, 4½"x7½", circa 1940s, Buzza, $20.00 – 40.00 (cb).

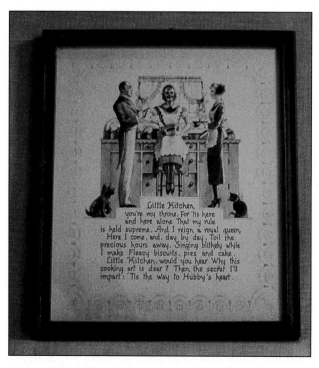

Print, 6½"x7½", circa 1940s, Buzza, $40.00 – 60.00 (cb)

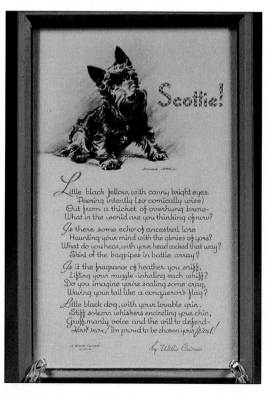

Print, 5¾"x8½", circa 1940s, Memory Keepsake, "Scottie" by Willis Cairness, art by Morgan Dennis, $40.00 – 60.00 (c).

Print, 5½"x6½", circa 1940s, Buzza, $25.00 – 40.00 (c).

Print, 5½"x6½", circa 1940s, Buzza, $30.00 – 50.00 (c).

Print, 6¾"x7¾", circa 1920 – 40s, Buzza, marked Copyright 1926, $30.00 – 50.00 (c).

Print, 4½"x4½", circa 1940s, Buzza, Artist: Aldin, left, Scotty; right, Sandy, $30.00 – 40.00 each (cb).

Print, 5½"x6½", circa 1940s, Buzza, $30.00 – 50.00 (c).

Print, 4¾"x5¾", $20.00 – 30.00 (cb).

Print, 10½"x12½", Artist: Corina, $40.00 – 60.00 (cb).

Print, 13"x15", Artist: Gear, marked Aberdeen Terrier, $80.00 – 120.00 (cb).

Print, 17½"x18½", circa 1947, Scotty #P511 October 1947, Artist: Cambler, $100.00 – 140.00 (cb).

Plaque, 4"x5", circa 1940s, Artist: Cambler, $20.00 – 40.00 (cb).

Print, "Check and Double Check," 11"x14", Artist: Grace Drayton for RKO Studios, circa 1930, $40.00 – 50.00 (p).

Print, 10"x13", circa 1944, Diana Thorne, $20.00 – 40.00 (c).

Print, 6¼"x4¼", circa 1930s, USAQ, $20.00 – 40.00 (cb).

Print, 5"x7", $30.00 – 50.00 (ch).

Print, 7"x9", Artist: Frances Tipron, "The Prize Winner," $15.00 – 30.00 (cb).

Photograph, 6"x8", circa 1930 – 40s, Jos. Manderfeld Co., Minn. USA, $30.00 – 40.00 (cb).

Print, pencil signed and titled, "The Pool," 8"x9", Artist: Marguerite Kirmse, circa 1930s, $250.00 – 400.00 (p).

Print, 9"x11", "Black and White," circa 1940, Artist: Morgan Dennis, $35.00 – 50.00 (p).

Plaque, 3¾"x5", "Playmates," circa 1930s, $15.00 (p).

Print, 8"x10", "Mac and Mike," $25.00 – 40.00 (ch).

Original Drawing, 8"x10½", circa 1940s, $40.00 – 60.00 (c).

Print, 10"x15", circa 1930s, by Gladys Emerson Cook, $30.00 – 50.00 (c).

Print, 8"x10", circa 1930s, "When Do We Eat?" by Morgan Dennis, $30.00 – 60.00 (c).

Print from Calendar, 8"x6", Artist: Elvgren, circa 1930s, $20.00 – 30.00 (p).

 150

Print, 8½"x10", "Midnight & Dawn" by A. Babcock, pencil signed and numbered block print, $125.00 – 175.00 (c).

Print, Limited Edition, 8"x10", "Black Bottom," pencil signed and numbered, 1990s, Artist: Marion Needham Krupp, $15.00 – 25.00 (c).

Print, Limited Edition, 8"x10", "Round the Christmas Tree," pencil signed and numbered, 1990s, Artist: Marion Needham Krupp, $15.00 – 25.00 (c).

Print, Limited Edition of 200, pencil signed and numbered, circa 1997, Artist: Kate Maynard, given to attendees of the 1997 Wee Scots Convention, no value determinable at this time (c).

Reverse Painting on Glass, 5"x7", circa 1930 – 40s, $30.00 – 50.00 (c).

Reverse Painting on Glass, 4"x6", circa 1930 – 40s, $30.00 – 50.00 (c).

Reverse Painting on Glass, 4"x5", circa 1930 – 40s, $30.00 – 50.00 (c).

Reverse Painting on Glass, 3"x4", circa 1930 – 40s, $30.00 – 50.00 (c).

Reverse Painting on Glass, 4"x5", circa 1930 – 40s, $30.00 – 50.00 (c).

MY DAILY PRAYER

Oh Lord help me keep my
Damn nose out of other
people's business.
--Amen.

Reverse Painting on Glass, 6½"x6½", circa 1930 – 40s, $30.00 – 50.00 (cb).

Reverse Painting on Glass, foil background, 3½"x3½", circa 1940s, $20.00 – 30.00 (p).

Reverse Painting on Glass, 4"x5", circa 1930s, marked Scotty Running, paired with Scotty Waiting, a silhouette of distinction from an old original hand cutting, uniquely transferred in enamels to glass preserving the full sharpness of detail. Another Reliance product, T-4, $25.00 – 35.00 (p).

Plaque, 8¼"x 11¼", brass, $40.00 – 60.00 (cb).

Reverse Painting on Glass, 4"x5", convex glass, circa 1940s, Benton Glass Co., $30.00 – 50.00 (p).

Toys and Games

The Scottie is known for his loyalty and steadfast companionship. What better image to use for a toy?

Stuffed, 13"x5"x10", mohair/straw stuffed, circa 1940s, wooden knob on chest causes head to swivel, $90.00 – 140.00 (c).

Stuffed, 6"x1¾"x4½", mohair/glass eyes, Steiff, Germany, $75.00 – 125.00 (cb).

Stuffed, 14", plush, 1990s, Douglas Cuddle Toys, $40.00 – 50.00 (p).

Mechanical, 10"x5"x7", short pile plush over metal frame, circa 1950s, battery operated causing leg and head movement, barking, and glowing eyes, $50.00 – 75.00 (c).

Stuffed, 11"x4"x8", mohair, German, $75.00 – 125.00 (cb).

Stuffed, 10½"x2½"x8", mohair, circa 1940s, $75.00 – 125.00 (cb).

Stuffed, 19"x5"x14", mohair, circa 1940s, Knickerbocker, marked NY USA, $100.00 – 150.00 (cb).

Pajama Bag, 24"x6½"x11", mohair, circa 1940 – 50s, Merry-thought, England, $75.00 – 125.00 (cb).

Stuffed, 12"x5"x9½", mohair/glass eyes/rubber nose and tongue, circa 1940s, USA, $75.00 – 120.00 (cb).

Puppet, 6"x7"x13", plush, 1990s, Country Critter's Inc., $25.00 – 30.00 (c). Available from FDR Museum Shop.

Stuffed, 2"x5"x3", plush, circa 1987, North American Bear Company, Muffy's dog "Scottie Vanderdog", $140.00 – 180.00 (c).

Stuffed, 10"x5"x6", plush, circa 1980s, premium with sleep shirt, $15.00 – 25.00 (c).

Stuffed, 11"x4"x8", rabbit fur, circa 1950s, $25.00 – 40.00 (c).

Beanie Baby, 3"x6"x6", plush/pellets, 1990s, Ty, $5.00 – 15.00 (c).

Stuffed, 7"x14"x9", plush, circa 1970s, handmade, $25.00 – 40.00 (c).

Stuffed, 9"x6"x16", plush/wool, 1990s, Cottage Collectibles by Ganz, #CC1203/McKenzie, China, $30.00 – 40.00 (c).

Stuffed, 6"x13"x11", plush, circa 1980s, "Duffy," Russ Berrier & Co. Inc., Korea, $20.00 – 30.00 (c).

Stuffed, 4¾"x2", manmade fibers, 1990s, Factoria Toyworks, USA, $65.00 – 85.00 each (cb).

Massager, 15"x8"x5", plush/cotton, circa 1980s, $15.00 – 25.00 (ch).

Stuffed, 5"x1¾"x3½", wool, circa 1940s, $40.00 – 60.00 (cb).

Stuffed, 6"x4"x8", plush, circa 1980s, North American Bear Company, Great Scot, squeaker, Korea, $20.00 – 40.00 each (c).

Stuffed, 4"x3"x3", plush, circa 1997, Cottage Collectibles by Ganz, #CC621 MacPherson, China, $12.00 – 15.00 (c).

Stuffed, left to right: 6"x7", mohair, childhood toy of Patty's cousin, circa 1940s, priceless; center and right, plush, 1990s, $20.00 – 30.00 (p).

Stuffed, plush, made for Harrods, distributed by QVC, 1990s, $25.00 (p).

Squeak Toys, 6" and 4", latex, circa 1950s, $5.00 – 10.00 (p).

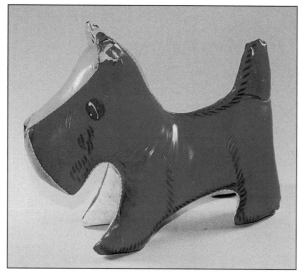

Stuffed, 4"x6"x7", vinyl, circa 1950s, $20.00 – 40.00 (c).

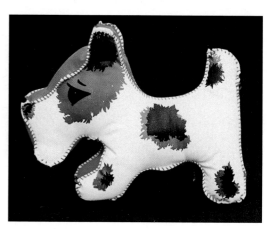

Stuffed Autograph Toy, 8"x9", vinyl, circa 1950s, $20.00 – 40.00 (p).

Stuffed, 6"x8"x9", vinyl, circa 1950s, $20.00 – 40.00 (c).

Mechanical, 11½"x3"x6", tin, Marx, USA, $200.00 – 300.00 (cb).

Stuffed, 4", leather, circa 1940s, $50.00 – 85.00 (p).

Mechanical Wind-Up, 3"x5", celluloid, circa 1920s, $90.00 – 100.00 (p).

Doll, 16", porcelain, 1990s, Lenox, Heather, $120.00 – 140.00 (ch).

Doll, 16", vinyl, 1990s, Spelling Fantasy Doll Inc., China, $130.00 – 160.00 (ch).

Left: Statue, 3"x4", chocolate glass, circa 1979, marked: RM St. Clair, Elwood, Indiana, 1979, $50.00 – 75.00; right: Candy Container, 3"x4", glass, circa 1940s, originally filled with colorful candy beads, $20.00 – 30.00 (p).

Pull Toy, 2½"x5"x4¼", composition wood/wood, circa 1946, Hubley, $50.00 – 75.00 (c).

Rubber Stamps, 1990s, $4.00 – 7.00 (p).

Pull Toy, 4"x7", advertising piece for Billiken Shoes, circa 1940s, $40.00 – 50.00 (p).

Pull Toy, 7¼"x2¾"x7", wood, circa 1950s, $20.00 – 40.00 (c).

Blocks, plastic, 1990s, Duplo, $20.00 – 25.00 (c).

Baby Rattle, 2" diameter, metal, circa 1930s, $40.00 – 60.00 (cb).

Pail, 8¼"x5¼"x4", metal, circa 1930s, $40.00 – 60.00 (cb).

Magnets, 1"x½", plastic, current, $5.00 – 10.00 (ch).

Music Box, 3¼"x3½", tin, circa 1930 – 40s, Wyandotte Toys, USA, $60.00 – 90.00 (cb).

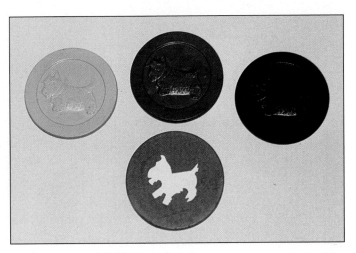

Poker Chips, 1½" diameter, clay, circa 1930 – 40s, $5.00 – 15.00 each (c).

Playing Cards, $10.00 – 30.00.
(Price per deck)

Playing Card Holder, shown closed, item below.

Playing Card Holder, 5"x6", wood/decal, circa 1950s,
$20.00 – 30.00 (p).

Playing Card Holder, 6"x4½"x2", composition wood, circa 1940s, Swank, USA, $20.00 – 30.00 (p).

Playing Card Holder, 4¾"x2½"x4", composition wood, circa 1940s, OrnaWood, $20.00 – 40.00 (c).

Playing Card Box, 5"x4"x3", composition wood, circa 1940s, SyrocoWood, $20.00 – 40.00 (c).

Spirits and Libations

With typical terrier spirit, we toast Scottie collectibles!

Decanter, 7"x4"x9", bone china, circa 1970, bottom marked Royal Adderley Floral Bone China Made in England, created exclusively for James Buchanan & Co. Ltd., Glasgow, Scotland, $50.00 – 75.00 (c).

Decanter, 5"x5"x10¼", bone china, Scotch original by Pemberton, USA, $25.00 – 50.00 (cb).

Display, 12", Black and White Scotch, bone china, not decanters but store display that looks like the decanters with non-removable heads, circa 1970, $50.00 – 75.00 each (p).

Scotch Bottle, B&W, 3½"x1½"x7¾", glass bottle/paper label, J. Buchanan & Co. Ltd., England, $25.00 – 40.00 (cb).

Flasks, 1½"x4"x6", glass/rubber covering, circa 1950s, $20.00 – 30.00 (cb).

Coaster, 3", paper, Black and White Scotch, $1.00 (p).

Jack in the Box with Plush Dogs, electric, Black and White Scotch. Dogs push their heads up, open the top of the box, bark, turn their heads, go back down, and the box closes. Circa 1970, Fleischmann Distributing Co., $150.00 – 350.00 (p).

Magazine Advertisement, 11"x14", Black and White Scotch, circa 1964, $3.00 – 7.00 (p).

Playing Cards, Black and White Scotch, circa 1970s, $5.00 – 20.00 (p).

Ashtray, 5½"x5½", ceramic, Black and White Scotch, James Gaffen and Nephew designers, Made in England, circa 1960s, $30.00 – 40.00 (p).

Pub Pitcher, 7", ceramic, Black and White Scotch, Heublein, Inc., circa 1974 – 84, $80.00 – 90.00 (p).

Bottle Display, 12"x12", molded plastic, Black and White Scotch, holds two bottles, circa 1970, $80.00 – 100.00 (p).

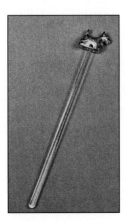

Swizzle Stick, glass/metal, $5.00 – 10.00 (c).

Mystery, 4"x2"x5", composition wood, $10.00 – 20.00 (c). Note: We have no idea what originally came in the opening in the back of this piece, but considering the subject matter, we thought it appropriate to include in this section.

Magazine Advertisement, 10"x13", Black and White Scotch, Artist: Morgan Dennis, Circa 1959, $3.00 – 7.00 (p).

Magazine Advertisement, Black and White Scotch, left: 5"x13", Artist: Morgan Dennis, circa 1952, $2.00 – 4.00; right: 5"x13", Artist: Morgan Dennis, circa 1946, $2.00 – 4.00 (p).

Magazine Advertisement, Black and White Scotch, left: 5"x13" Artist: Morgan Dennis, circa 1946 $2.00 – 4.00; right: 5"x13", circa 1944, $2.00 – 4.00 (p).

Magazine Advertisements, Black and White Scotch, left: 5"x13", Artist: Morgan Dennis, circa 1952, $2.00 – 4.00; right: 5"x13", Artist: Morgan Dennis, circa 1952, $2.00 – 4.00 (p).

Magazine Advertisements, Black and White Scotch, left: 5"x13", circa 1955, $2.00 – 4.00; right, 5"x13", Artist: Morgan Dennis, circa 1954, $2.00 – 4.00 (p).

Magazine Advertisements, Black and White Scotch, left: 5"x13", Artist: Morgan Dennis, circa 1955, $2.00 – 4.00; right: 5"x13", Artist: Morgan Dennis, circa 1955, $2.00 – 4.00 (p).

Magazine Advertisement, Black and White Scotch, left: 5"x13", Artist: Morgan Dennis, circa 1957, $2.00 – 4.00; right: 5"x13", circa 1950, $2.00 – 4.00 (p).

Magazine Advertisement, 10"x13", Black and White Scotch, Artist: Morgan Dennis, circa 1957, $3.00 – 7.00 (p).

Magazine Advertisement, *Fortune*, 10"x13", Black and White Scotch, circa 1952, $3.00 – 7.00(p).

Magazine Advertisement, 10"x13", Black and White Scotch, Artist: Morgan Dennis, circa 1950, $3.00 – 7.00 (p).

Magazine Advertisement, Black and White Scotch, left: 5"x13", Artist: Morgan Dennis, circa 1950, $2.00 – 4.00; right: 5"x13", circa 1955, $2.00 – 4.00 (p).

Scottie Sightings

In the Movies

Though rarely the star, the Scottish terrier and Scottie collectibles appear in the motion pictures. Here are a few where we have spotted our favorite fellow.

"Angus Lost" — a starring role
"Another Thin Man" — he's definitely a rogue in this one
"Forsaking All Others" — just a bit part
"Groundhog Day" — watch the windowsill near the beginning
"Kennel Murder Case, The" — they're everywhere
"Lady and the Tramp" — best supporting actor award here
"Light That Failed, The" — drama for sure
"McHale's Navy Joins the Air Force" — cameo as Fala
"Men In Black" — fireplace scene
"Stand-In, The" — Bogart's companion

Recently a Scottie was spotted in a Monopoly Brothers advertisement on television. You never know when or where these little fellows will raise their little pointed ears and make a guest appearance!

In Books and Old Readers

Books

This collection lists titles, authors, and illustrators of just a small sampling of books with an emphasis on Scottie dogs.

ABC Dogs	Tice, Clara	Tice, Clara
All About Pets	Bianco, Margery Williams	Gilkison, Grace
Angus and the Cat	Flack, Marjorie	Flack, Marjorie
Angus and the Ducks	Flack, Marjorie	Flack, Marjorie
Angus Lost	Flack, Marjorie	Flack, Marjorie
Animals (cloth)		
Best Dog Stories	Various	Various
Black Rod	Poultney, C.B.	Poultney, C.B.
Bonnie Bits O' Bonnie Scotland	Junior, Allan	
Book of the Scottish Terrier 1948	Ewing, Fayette	
Child's Book of Dogs, A	Henderson, Luis M.	Henderson, Luis M.
Child's Garden of Verses, A	Stevenson, Robert Louis	Trimmer, George
Chipper	Whitman Publishers	
Code of the Woosters, The	Wodehouse, P.G.	
Complete Scottish Terrier 1976	Marvin, John T.	
Crazy Quilt Circus Pony	Brown, Paul	Brown, Paul
Dabble Duck	Ellis, Anne Leo	Truesdell, Sue
Dog Book, The	Terhune, Albert Payson	Thorne, Diana
Dog Friends	Scott, A.O.	Scott, A.O.
Dog Stories	Held, John Jr.	Held, John Jr.
Dogs	Dennis, Morgan	Dennis, Morgan
Dogs As I See Them	Dawson, Lucy	Dawson, Lucy
Dogs Rough and Smooth	Dawson, Lucy	Dawson, Lucy
Dogs, An Album of Drawings	Thorne, Diana	Thorne, Diana
Dogs, Paintings and Stories	Thorne, Diana	Thorne, Diana
Drawing Dogs	Cook, Gladys Emerson	Cook, Gladys Emerson
Eric Gurney's Pop-Up Book of Dogs		Eric Gurney
Fala Factor, The	Kaminsky, Stuart M.	
Falla A President's Dog	Mussey, Virginia Howell	Van Doren, Margaret

amous Dog Stories	Various	Stover, Wallace
amous Mascots & K-9s	Harmer, Mabel	
lover's Dog Book 1937		
ollywood Dogs	Suares, J.C.	
ow to Raise and Train a Scottish Terrier 1960	Gannon, Robert	VanDerMeid, Louise
ust Pups	Barker, K.F.	Barker, K.F.
ittle Golden Book of Dogs	Jones, Nita	Gergely, Tibor
1ac Goes to School	Wynkoop, Margaret L.	Richie, Robert Yarnell
1y Story – The Official Fala Coloring Book		
obody's Doll	DeLeeuw, Adele	Vaughn, Anne
eggy Brown & the Big Haunted House	Heinsenfelt, Kathryn	Vallely, Henry
eggy Brown & the Jewel of Fire	Heinsenfelt, Kathryn	Vallely, Henry
eggy Brown & the Mystery Basket	Heinsenfelt, Kathryn	Vallely, Henry
eggy Brown & the Runaway Auto Trailer	Heinsenfelt, Kathryn	Vallely, Henry
eggy's Pokey and Other Stories		Malvern, Corrine
et Scottish Terrier 1958	Snethen, Mr. & Mrs. T.H.	Dennis, Morgan
ete	Robinson, Tom	Dennis, Morgan
ets a Sit in Panorama	Kalab, Theresa	Kalab, Theresa
ets at the Whitehouse	Carmer, Carl	Savitt, Sam
laytime Paint Book	Whitman Publishers	
ortrait of a Dog	DeLaRoche, Mazo	Dennis, Morgan
resident FDR and Best Friend Fala Coloring Book	Diana, Darling	
and McNally Junior Elf	Stahlmann, Catherine	Wilde, Irma
ubaiyat of a Scotch Terrier	Collins, Sewell	Collins, Sewell
cotch Dhu	Poultney, C.B.	Poultney, C.B.
ergeant's Dog Book 1945	Dennis, Morgan	Dawson, Lucy
here Was Tammie	Bryan, Dot & Marg	Bryan, Dot & Marg
hy Servant a Dog	Kipling, Rudyard	Kirmse, Marguerite
hy Servant a Dog	Kipling, Rudyard	Stampa, G.L.
rue Story of Fala, The	Suckley, Margaret and Dalgliesh, Alice	Fairchild, E.N.
Vaggery Town	Duncan, Philip	Duncan, Philip
Vhere are you?	See, Sam	Lieberman, Frank
Vorld Book of Dogs	Tatham, Julie Campbell	Megergee, Edwin

Old Readers

ll Around Us	Beauchamp, Wilbur L.	
long The Way	Hildreth, Gertrude	Berry, Erick; Chapman, F.T.; Esley, Joan
t Play	Hildreth, Gertrude	Waterall, Corrine Pauli
ay In and Day Out	O'Donnell, Mabel	Hoopes, Florence & Margaret; Carey, Alice
own the River Road	O'Donnell, Mabel	Hoopes, Florence & Margaret
Know A Secret	Hildreth, Gertrude	Waterall, Corrine Pauli, Abott, Jacob B.
ittle Dog Lost	Wright, Lula	Winifred Bromhall
1ac and Muff	Hildreth, Gertrude	Waterall, Corrine Pauli
1ore Streets and Roads	Gray, William S.	Arbuthnot, May Hill
n Four Feet	Gates, Arthur I.	Huber, Miriam Blanton; Salisbury, Frank S.
ets and Play Times	Grady, William E.	Hoopes, Florence; Freeman, Margaret
hrough the Gate	Various	Holland, Janice; Tate, Sally
oday We Go	Gates, Arthur I.	Huber, Miriam Blanton; Salisbury, Frank S.
Ve Are Neighbors	Ousley, Odille	

173

Scottie Publications

Scottie Sampler – A Guide To Scottie Dog Collectibles

The *Scottie Sampler* has been a quarterly publication since 1983. Each issue includes feature stories, historical data, photos, advertisements, and current prices of Scottie collectibles. The annual subscription rate is $22.00 in the United States, Canada, and Mexico. All other foreign subscriptions are $34.00.

Scottie Sampler sponsors an annual collectors' convention for magazine subscribers, the group known as "Wee Scots." The June 1997 convention saw 192 people come together for three days of education, fellowship, and acquisition and marked the twelfth time Wee Scotters have met nationally. There are also numerous regional meetings around the United States in which Wee Scotters actively participate.

For subscription information, contact DBDesigns, Dept. 56, PO Box 2597, Winchester, VA 22604-1797, or e-mail bohnlein@shentel.net, or phone 540-662-6968.

Great Scots Magazine - Celebrating Scotties and Their People

Great Scots Magazine has been a bi-monthly publication since January 1996. Published by The Tartan Scottie, each issue features articles about the Scottish terrier, centering on the relationship between Scotties and their people. Publisher Joseph G. Harvill and partner Charlotte J. Harvill have given us a wealth of information on this very special terrier breed, including ways to improve our Scottie's health and well being. Though not specifically published for the Scottie collector, every issue offers a variety of items to add to your accumulation.

Annual subscription rate is $18.00 (USA), $30.00 (foreign). Please contact The Editor, 1028 Girard N.E., Albuquerque, NM 87106, or e-mail scottie@nmia.com, or phone 505-266-7211.

Scottie Merchandisers

Scotty's Gifts & Accessories, 3802 Ivey Lane, Lilburn, GA 30047-2134, 1-800-638-2338, e-mail: Scotty-LuvR@scottysgifts.com

Scot's Ahoy, 211 Grandview Drive, Suite 101, Ft. Mitchell, KY 41017, 1-888-726-8246, web site: www.scotsahoy.com

Campbell's Scottish Terriers, 10710 Almond Street, Fairfax, VA 22032, 1-703-591-5253, e-mail: KidfixerC3@aol.com

Tartan Scottie, 1028 Girard NE, Albuquerque, NM 87106, 1-800-766-6091, e-mail: scottie@nmia.com

Biscotti's Boutique, 6 Carter Street, Hanover, NH 03755, designs by Martha Lorden

DB Designs, P.O.B. 2597, Winchester, VA 22604-1797, 1-540-662-4272, e-mail bohnlein@shentel.net

Wilderstein, Friends of Fala, P.O. Box 383, Rhinebeck, NY 12572, 1-914-876-4818

FDR Library, The Museum Store, 511 Albany Post Road, Hyde Park, NY 12538, 1-800-FDR-VISIT

Tinkers Treasures, 35609 Persimmon St., Yucaipa, CA 92399, 1-909-797-6982

Theresa's Treasures, P.O. Box 103, Slaterville Springs, NY 14881, e-mail: TheresaT@clarityconnect.com

In The Company of Dogs, P.O. Box 7071, Dover, DE 19903, 1-800-924-5050

Puttin' On The Dog, 5140 Shadow Path Lane, Lilburn, GA 30247-7703, 1-800-720-8005, web site: www.puttinonthedog.com

The Dog's House, 2511 Irving Road, Thaxton, VA 24174, 1-800-851-6899

Bibliography

Dale, Jean. *The Charlton Standard Catalogue of Royal Doulton Animals, 1st Ed.*, Toronto, Canada: The Charlton Press, 1994.

Florence, Gene. *The Collector's Encyclopedia of Akro Agate, Revised Ed.*, Paducah, Kentucky: Collector Books, 1992.

Florence, Gene. *The Collector's Encyclopedia of Depression Glass, 12th Ed.*, Paducah, Kentucky: Collector Books, 1996.

Garmon, Lee and Dick Spencer. *Glass Animals of the Depression Era*, Paducah, Kentucky: Collector Books, 1993.

Gibbs, Carl Jr. *Collector's Encyclopedia of Metlox Potteries, Identification and Values*, Paducah, Kentucky: Collector Books, 1995.

Hall, Doris and Burdell. *Morton Potteries: 99 Years, Vol. 2*, Gas City, Indiana: L-W Book Sales, 1995.

Huxford, Sharon and Bob, Ed. *Schroeder's Antiques Price Guide, 15th Ed.*, Paducah, Kentucky: Collector Books, 1997.

Jones, Van. *J.B. Color Chart, Scottie Sampler*, Winchester, Virginia: DB Designs, Volume 14, Number 1, November, 1996, 7.

Lehner, Lois. *Lehner's Encyclopedia of U.S. Marks on Pottery, Porcelain, and Clay*, Paducah, Kentucky: Collector Books, 1988.

Nissen, Craig and Bob and Margaret Hanson. *McCoy Pottery, Collector's Reference and Value Guide*, Paducah, Kentucky: Collector Books, 1997.

Seecof, Donna and Robert and Louis Kuritzky. *Bookend Revue*, Atglen, Pennsylvania: Schiffer Publishing, 1996.

Sherwood, Stephanie. *"Scottie Soldiers," Scottie Sampler*, Winchester, Virginia: DB Designs, Volume 7, Number 3, Spring, 1990.

Weatherman, Hazel Marie. *Colored Glassware of the Depression Era 2*, Ozark, Missouri: Glassbooks, 1974.

Weatherman, Hazel Marie. *The Decorated Tumbler*, Springfield, Missouri: Glassbooks, Inc., 1978.

White, Carol Bess. *Made in Japan Ceramics*, Paducah, Kentucky: Collector Books, 1996.

Whitmeyer, Margaret and Kenn. *Bedroom and Bathroom Glassware of the Depression Years*, Paducah, Kentucky: Collector Books, 1990.

Whitmeyer, Margaret and Kenn. *Collector's Encyclopedia of Children's Dishes*, Paducah, Kentucky: Collector Books, 1995.

Wisniewski, Debra J. *Antique & Collectible Buttons*, Paducah, Kentucky: Collector Books, 1997.